Hints On the Formation of Gardens and Pleasure Grounds

003180652
rev. 4.21.2003

CONTENTS.

CONTENTS.

CHAP. VII.

INTRODUCTION.

In submitting to the public eye a work of the present description, it may be expected that some reason would be assigned for offering it at the present time. The author would therefore state, that the subjects of this volume have been almost wholly overlooked by the modern writers on laying out grounds. The progress of the art developed in the present volume, has, during the last century, been extended from a few acres near the house, to the whole of an extensive domain; its practice, from an arbitrary disposition of forms borrowed from the architecture of the mansion, or the alleys and slopes of the kitchen garden, to a display of expression or character, indicated by the situation, and suitable to the purposes in view. The vast field thus opened to the artist has directed his attention to the study of natural landscape, and generalized his views of artificial scenery: while his practical efforts, influenced by the bias of his studies, have been chiefly conspicuous on extensive scenes; where he has improved, more with reference to the effect of the whole, than to the excellence of the smaller parts; more with an eye to the picturesque beauty of the

b

landscape, than to the excellence of the kitchen garden, or the farm, the comfort and neatness of the parterre, the shrubbery, or the green-house.

It follows, that small spots, from being less adapted to this system of improvement, and the detail of country seats in general, from being less the subject of the artist's studies, have been completely neglected. Thus, while quartos and folios have been sent forth on landscape gardening, picturesque improvements, or country residences, we have been upwards of a century without seeing any work to supersede the ancient plans and treatises on parterres and kitchen gardens, by Switzer and Le Bond; or the " Gardens for the Town," by Batty Langley, Le Meagre, and others.

The designs in those works being wholly adapted for clipt trees, shorn hedges, and groves, are too obsolete, as well as too expensive in execution, for the present day. The prevailing taste, however, must be imitated; the modern style, therefore, has been applied in town villas without science, and the grounds of the retiring citizen filled up with clumps and strips of trees, after the undigested ideas of his builder or upholsterer; or planted out with borders of rare shrubbery, by his nurseryman. Such is the general taste in the vicinity of the metropolis: however, there are a number of exceptions, which prove that taste may display itself to advantage, where there is neither great extent to work on, nor an immense sum to be expended.

It is natural for a mind unacquainted with the powers of art, to suppose that professional assistance can effect little in laying out small gardens or places of a few acres; but this is to infer, that nothing can be beautiful that is not also extensive. Beauty or expression depend no more on dimension than on expence, but are the result of a combination of parts forming a whole, calculated by its fitness and utility to gratify the mind, and by its effect to charm the eye. The rules for the formation of such combinations in rural scenery, constitute the art of laying out grounds; in the application of which, to a small place, the artist will often meet with difficulties unknown in places of greater extent; since these, by their magnitude, naturally possess a certain greatness of character; while a small spot is a blank, depending for its effect wholly on the skill and ingenuity of him who undertakes to fill it up.

Among the plans both for small places, gardens, and parterres, submitted in the following pages, are some in the ancient geometrical style of rural improvement. After this style has been a century laid aside, it may require some apology for attempting to revive it.

In the first place, Gardens, parterres, and such small subjects as are seen at one view, and in which symmetry, or at least undisguised art, must necessarily appear, bear with them their own apology. They are, and must always be, characterised by avowed art of some description: by giving examples of the

ancient mode of displaying this avowed art, as well as specimens
in the modern manner, a greater source of variety is obtained.

Secondly, The application of the geometrical style to
places of several acres, is, at first sight, less defensible, and at
all events is more obnoxious to modern taste: but it is only
proposed to introduce this style occasionally, and that in flat
or level situations, having little or no distant prospect, and no
facilities or capability for the modern style; every unpreju-
diced amateur in rural affairs will allow, that in such situations
this style produces a more marked and imposing character than
the modern style admits of, and tends also to vary the appearance of a flat country. It is the peculiar property of the modern
style, to heighten the natural character of a varied surface; but
in a flat situation it can effect nothing, but simple variety.

It is the peculiar property of the geometrical character to
counteract the natural indications of the surface, and confer its
own character; and in a flat it is all powerful; it has nothing to
oppose it; the Gothic mansion rears its formal, but majestic
front, and flings around its stately mantle of alleys, avenues,
and groves. Thus, the principle on which is recommended the
occasional introduction of this style, *wholly* on flats, and *par-*
tially in some more varied situations, is, *that a marked character,*
though formal and unnatural, is more interesting than an insipid
expression or no character at all.

What can be more insipid than an extensive flat without

water or old trees, bounded on all sides by low grounds, affording no distant prospect, but the hedge, or the belt that forms the boundary to the whole? Modern gardening can make little impression on such a scene. It may vary it with groups, and thickets of trees, and thereby render it pleasing and picturesque throughout; but in this uniform variety there will be a general monotony and want of character, and the defects of a flat, will be every where conspicuous. It belongs to the geometric style to create a bold and imposing grandeur, which will leave no room to regret the want of variety of surface or of distant prospect.

It is only necessary to recal to the memory Chatsworth, the magnificent seat of the Duke of Devonshire, in Derbyshire; Hampton Court, and Bushey Park, in Middlesex; Powis Castle, in Montgomeryshire; and Lowther Hall, in Westmoreland; to know what can be effected by this style, either when wholly prevalent, as in the two former places, or (as in the two latter), partially introduced by way of contrast to the wildness and luxuriance of romantic landscape.

The Regent's Park, the magnificent design of the late Mr. Fordyce, Surveyor General, now executing in Marylebone Farm, will in a few years afford a noble example of the union of the ancient and modern styles of planting. From what is already done, and from the particular facilities of the soil and situation, the architect has an opportunity of combining the

grandeur of avenues, open groves, and circular platoons of wood,
with the variety of light groups, close thickets, and single
trees, to introduce episodes or *bye-scenes* of wildness and rude
scenery, by planting spaces of rough ground with thorns, furze,
briars, brambles, ferns and heath; and others of the most refined elegance, by the prevalence, in glades, of smoothly mown
turf of the most elegant, delicate, or showy exotics.

Respecting the designs for kitchen gardens and glass houses,
or frames, given in this work, it is to be observed, that of many
recent discoveries, none connected with the subject that have
been *tried and known* are omitted.   One innovation in the construction of hot houses—the use of copper sashes and iron rafters
instead of wood—deserved to be mentioned, as the greatest improvement hitherto made in horticultural architecture.

The several lists of trees, shrubs, and flowers, priced and characterised, which constitute the last chapter of this work, by
enabling amateurs to select their plants from something more
than mere names, will promote the introduction of a more judi-
cious variety in ornamental plantations.   Those shrubs, which
require a particular soil, are marked in one of the lists; and
the homely phrase of gardeners need hardly be added, that
where the soil cannot be produced for the plants, the plants
should be adapted to the soil.   If this be neglected, their growth
is stinted and their foliage assumes a sickly hue, hardly to be
compensated by the variety of the species even to botanists,

4

and at all events less pleasing to the general observer, than the luxuriance of the common and showy sorts. These plants and trees, which ought to form the principals in every extensive plantation, if not for permanent use, at least for present effect, and shelter, have the threefold advantage of being easily obtained at any nursery; at most nurseries of a large size, so as to produce effect at once, and at all they are of a moderate price.

The introduction of rare plants, however, deserves every encouragement in extensive shrubberies, especially in the front of thickets, near walks, and in every situation where they are likely to attract the eye of the rural lounger. Whatever has a tendency to promote the study of the vegetable kingdom cannot be indifferent to those, who derive from plants either directly or indirectly the chief comforts of human life. In this respect, new objects of study may excite new desires in the student.

The display of a superior taste in the small places and garden scenes, discussed in this work, appears to the author to be called for by the general progress of the age. From the expence of consulting eminent professors in this line, many are deterred from applying for their aid. Nurserymen and builders, therefore, have been necessitated to supply their places, and it is for their aid, as well as for the information of the amateur who lays out his own grounds, that the author of this work submits it to the candid examination of an impartial public.

London, March 23, 1812.

PLANS

LAYING OUT PLEASURE GROUNDS, &c.

CHAP. I.

Observations on the Mode of laying out small Plots of Ground,
from one Perch to an Acre, in extent; referring to Plates I.
II. III. IV. and V.

THE common mode of laying out spaces of this description
in figures and compartments, after the manner of parterres,
seems so well adapted for the purpose in view, as to direct any
attempt at improvement chiefly to the variation of the figures.
The artificial forms displayed in gardens of this description harmonize with their artificial situation, and in limits so confined,
are more interesting than either an attempt to produce grandeur,
or to imitate the simplicity of rural nature. Where singularity
is aimed at, however, or in particular cases and situations, it
may be proper to deviate from general rules and ideas, and introduce either some grotesque or uncommon work of art, or
a portion of picturesque, or even rude scenery, one of the
public squares, laid out with an irregular surface, covered by

B

heath, and varied by furze, brambles, hollies, thorns, briars, ferns, thistles, with rocky pits or dingles, and in place of covered seats, mud huts, or turf hovels, would certainly possess a striking character, when contrasted with the tasteful elegance of others. The occasional introduction of a similar style might be admitted in the embellishment of small ground plots, with considerable effect, but it should be used sparingly.

The gardens of this description are usually of three sorts: 1. Such as are composed of turf, dug work, and gravel ; 2. Such as have gravel and dug work only ; and, 3. Those which require carriage entrances.

Pl. I. Contains fourteen designs for gardens of the first des-cription, where the compartments of flowers are raised or formed out of a ground· or surface of turf, and the walks of gravel, edged with the same material. This class is the least costly to execute, but the most expensive to preserve, from the necessity of frequent mowing. The situation for their adoption must be airy, and the soil under the turf poor, as it is only under such circumstances that the turf will assume a close velvet appearance, which, with the pleasing expanse of green, renders gardens of this description so superior to those of gravel and earth only.

Pl. II. Contains twelve designs for laying out plots composed of earth and gravel; the compartments for flowers having their edgings or margins formed by plants adapted for that purpose, as box, thrift, daisy, &c. This mode is the most generally applicable in towns, and by far the most economical to preserve in order; nothing more being necessary than to pull out weeds, and stir the earth once or twice a year. The examples in this plate, together with the figures in Plate I. will suggest a thousand other forms, adapted for similar purposes.

PLATE III.

Contains four designs which apply to plots somewhat larger, or from two to ten perches.

Fig. 1. Exhibits a circle containing a piece of water, which, as it is intended to be seen only from the house, is therefore placed on one side of the space, with a back ground of trees. This device serves to increase the apparent size of the circle; while the trees, by preventing the eye from seeing the entrance-gate from the house, and the whole plot from any point of view, leaves room for the imagination to magnify its extent.

a. Compartments of dug work, cut in the turf in the French style, for flowering plants, roses, and tender shrubs.

b. Trees and evergreen shrubs, with some deciduous sorts grouped throughout the turf, so as to throw it into bays and recesses of irregular size, shape, and situation; a few tall growing plants, as aster, hollyhock, pæony, astragalis, &c. may be introduced among the groups, and some early blowing bulbs in the turf.

Fig. 2. Shews the joint plot of two houses, which have their doors at *a a.*

b. Borders of dug work on turf in the ancient English style of gardening, as delineated by Le Meagre, in his Designs for Parterres and Patch-work.

c. Baskets of flowers or roses; the baskets of wicker or lattice work, constructed of cast iron, or wood well painted.

Fig. 3. A design in the French style, intermingled with what may be called the picturesque manner; part of the lawn, or turf, being covered with irregular tufts, or picturesque patches, of strawberries, camomile, primroses, creeping thyme, daisy,

&c. &c. interspersed with groups of tall growing plants and shrubs.

a. Picturesque patches. *b.* Baskets of flowers.

c. Shell work, as in French parterres (see Chap. IV.), or flints, scoriæ of metals, spars, &c. may be substituted in the manner of rock work, and either left naked, or covered with mountain plants, as saxifrages, alchemillas, thymes, cistuses, &c.

d. Dry patches and compartments for elegant shrubs and flowering plants.

Fig. 4. Is a design, in which the entrance is intended to be private, and is therefore concealed by,

a. A hedge. *b.* Entrance hall. *c.* Billiard room. *d.* Library.

e. Glass varandah to the library. (For a plan and elevation of a glass varandah, see Pl. XX.)

f. Borders of dug work on turf, in the modern style, intended to render it inconvenient for spectators to step into the lawn and so recognize the extent and shape of,

g. The water, of a picturesque shape, and natural character, with its boundaries concealed by trees, &c.

PLATE IV.

Contains four designs, in the same class as the last described plate.

Fig. 1. A plan in the modern style, for a plot of ten perches in the suburbs of a town.

a. Entrance to the house. *b.* Covered seats.

c. Large cages for singing or other curious birds, which may frequently be introduced, with excellent effect, in small spots of this description.

d. Baskets of roses, or carnations, or other rare or showy flowers.

e. Baskets, or dug compartments, for flowers and flowering shrubs.

The groups of trees and shrubs in these designs require no explanation; bulbs, as crocus, snowdrop, &c. are always supposed introduced in the lawn in small plots of this description.

Fig. 2. Is in the old English style, with a slight admixture of the modern in the grouping of the trees.

a. Principal entrance. *b.* Offices of business.

c Conservatory or kitchen. *d.* Baskets of flowers.

e. Compartments of dug work.

f. Beds of earth, with small sea shells strewed over the surface; these beds are for bulbous roots in spring, and tender annual flowers in summer.

g. Trees cut into pyramids, and other fanciful shapes.

h. Trees and shrubs grouped in the modern manner, and in their natural shapes.

Fig. 3. A design in the French and picturesque styles intermingled.

a. Gravel. *b.* Turf. *c.* Dug work. *d.* Shell work.

e. Clipt trees, planted in beds of curious shells or stones.

f. Shrubs in their natural state. *g.* Edging of flowers.

h. Hedges cut into pilasters, niches, and other compartments.

i. Natural thorns, holly, and briars, with cages for birds hung on them, &c.

Fig. 4. A design in the modern style.

a. The dug work, either enclosed in baskets, or left plain.

b. Gravel with turf edges.

c. Lawn, interspersed with trees and shrubs, deciduous and. evergreen.

PLATE V.

Contains two designs for eight perches. Fig. 1. and 2. in airy open situations, in wide streets, or in the suburbs, having the passage or walk from the street to the house covered with glass; and two designs for grounds with carriage entrances of twelve perches extent.

Fig. 1. Is a design calculated for gravel and earth without turf. The entrance in cold or wet weather may be underneath

a. The glass varandah, on which roses and vines are trained; and in mild weather along,

b. The open gravel walks.

c. Beds of flowers in the modern English style.

d. Shrubbery and flowering plants in the same style.

e. Edgings of flowers.

Instead of glass, common trellis work, covered with creepers, or the modern varandah roof, may be used; but glass is greatly to be preferred, on account of its admitting light, to promote the growth of vines or creepers, which form a much more agreeable shade than the dull uniformity of a dark roof.

Fig. 2. A design intended for entrance, either by a conservatory or glass varandah, or an open walk, and with the parterre chiefly composed of lawn and dug work.

a. Porch. *b.* Vestibule. *c.* Dining-room. *d.* Drawing-room.

e. Billiard-room. *f.* Library. *g.* Conservatory.

h. Dug borders with edgings of flowers.

i. Turf with baskets or dug compartments.

k. Lawn interspersed with variegated box, laurel, and hollies.

l. Open gravel walk. *m.* Outer porch.

The most delicate plants of the conservatory are proposed to be placed opposite the dining and billiard rooms, the fires of which will serve to heat that part of it to a sufficient temperature; the other parts will be devoted to hardier sorts, requiring protection from cold, rather than artificial heat, such as myrtles, geraniums, roses, vines, hydrangias, &c. which in the south of England the glass will sufficiently protect from the external air in frosty weather.

Fig. 3. Is a design adapted to the entrance of carriages from the street to the door of the house.

a. House. *b.* Stables.

c. Lawn; trees and shrubs, with furze, thorns, hollies, &c. in the forest style; but without flowers or very rare shrubs, which on an entrance front of a mansion are too refined for the situation.

d. Path round to the garden front of the house, and to the water closet, if that appendage is not within the house.

Fig. 4. A design of the same character as the last, where the entrance to the stables is by,

a. A separate lane for servants, &c.

b. A piece of picturesque water.

c. An ascent by which carriages drive under the portico: a very material comfort, both in town and country houses.

d. The portico, the floor of which is about three feet above the level of the water.

These two designs are supposed to have parterres in the other front of the house.

In several of the designs described in this chapter, water is introduced; a feature which in London, from the recent supplies by new companies, may be obtained in abundance at a moderate price. Aquatic plants and drooping trees are

the natural accompaniments of water, and in artificial scenery
the more elegant and select sorts, as nymphæa, alisma, weeping willow, weeping birch, &c. ought occasionally to be introduced in the margins of pools, both of formal and picturesque
shapes. They give an air of truth and nature to those scenes,
which ought never to be dispensed with, when it can be obtained.

In many of the designs, trees are shewn as if planted in the
sides of the walks, and close by the houses or boundary walls.
This communicates a free unconstrained effect, and gains room
for trees, and an appearance of woodiness, at little expence of
lawn or dug ground, which in small spots is both convenient
and pleasing.

It is needless to say much as to the trees to be used in situations such as have been described, since every species may occasionally be introduced; but in small spots, such deciduous
sorts as have a great abundance of spray and twigs, as the
lime and the beech, are much to be preferred to those that are
deficient in these respects, as the ash and the alder. The stone
and cluster pine are the noblest evergreens that can be introduced; but the air of cities frequently does not agree with
them; hollys, evergreen oaks, and a few other sorts, are most
to be depended on.

Of the flowering plants and shrubs, some ought to be introduced of each colour of blossom, and for every month in the
year; or at all events for those months when the family
occupy the mansion. A proper selection may readily be made
from the lists in chapter VII.

CHAP. II.

On laying out the Grounds of Villas, from one to one hundred Acres in extent, referring to Plates VI. VII. VIII. IX. and X.

Places of this extent afford the artist some opportunity of displaying his taste and ingenuity; his taste in inventing an appropriate design, and his ingenuity in devising expedients for carrying it into execution.

In forming a design for any situation, the first thing the artist ought to be made acquainted with, is the purpose and wants of the proprietor. Whether he intends it as a winter, summer, constant, or occasional residence; the number of his domestic circle, the style of his society, and general scale of expenditure. These things being given, together with the situation, the first business is, either of himself or in conjunction with an architect, (according to his knowledge in architecture, or the wishes of his employer), to devise a proper plan for a new house, or adequate additions to the edifice that may be existing on the grounds. If a new house is to be built, the first point to determine, is the most eligible spot on which to erect it; in which a due regard must be paid to the several requisites of shelter from winds, exposure to the sun, dry foundations, good water, declivity for drainage, distant views, trees which may already exist on the spot, proper distance from the boundary of the estate, facility of approach, &c. &c.

The situation of the house being fixed on, next in order comes its accommodations and domestic conveniencies; then the quantity of stabling and other offices, as well as the extent of kitchen

C

garden and farming ground, (if any), suitable to the wants of the family. In arranging these requisites, it will generally be found desirable, especially in small places, to have the stabling near the house, and on the side or wing in which the kitchen and other offices are situated ; and also that this side or wing should be nearest the entrance lodge or outer gate, in order that servants approaching the kitchen, or that any intercourse with the stables, may take place without the parties passing in front of the sitting rooms. On the same side with the stables and offices, should, for similar reasons, be placed the kitchen garden, and especially for the conveyance of manure, unseen from the living rooms of the house.

It may be observed, that in some situations these points cannot be attended to, especially when a house is to be enlarged or altered; but in such cases, by a proper arrangement of the living rooms, the inconvenience alluded to may be in a great measure avoided. It need scarcely be stated, that in every case the stables and offices should be so far embosomed in wood as to conceal partially their architecture, and wholly the routine of domestic affairs.

These points being settled, the artist will next proceed to consider what extent of walk will be suitable to the family, what the place will admit of, and what its distant prospects, home views, or internal beauties, indicate. These circumstances duly weighed will naturally lead him to form an adequate plan for the walks in the grounds near the house, and those at a distance; and to decide whether the situation, and the taste of the family, require the grounds to be set off with artificial decoration, or whether its natural beauties will not, with some improvements and additions, have the better effect. All these points having been considered with reference to the nature of the soil, situation, and intended expenditure, an important point still remains to be adjusted. It is not enough to know the spot on which the house is to be built, or the accomodation requisite both in the house and the grounds. The STYLE in which the whole is to be designed and executed must be determined on. It is true this is a matter little thought of in general; a proper idea of the necessity of one style or character pervading not only the house, but every part of a place, seldom entering into the minds either of proprietors or artists. No design combining taste with use can be deemed perfect, however, till this is attended to; for wherever pleasing sentiments are to be excited in the human mind, it must heighten the effect of such sentiments when they have a common alliance among themselves. In those arts, the principal object of which is to delight, such as poetry, painting, and music, the want of this principle is instantly felt; in the art of laying out grounds also, though a useful as well as pleasing art, it should be the aim of the artist, not merely to create such parts as are essential to comfort and convenience, or bring together an assemblage of pleasing scenery, but to form such an arrangement of objects, as, besides their use, will raise at once some precise characteristic emotion or expression, and support the same sentiment throughout.

From these remarks some idea may be formed of what is intended by style, and to what extent this idea should be carried where perfection is aimed at. The grand foundation for adopting a style is the natural character previously existing; for example, where a romantic, a grand, or a simple style of landscape prevails: but even in small spots, such as are immediately alluded to, much may be done by preserving the same style of building and planting, the same prevailing trees and shrubs, and the same proportion of parts, as roads, walks, &c.

throughout the whole. It may be observed, that this must be less difficult to effect, where a strongly marked artificial style is adopted, such as the geometric or ancient mode of gardening, than where a more simple and natural style is attempted without any marked indications of nature.

These remarks would have been better illustrated by views and sections of grounds and scenery than by the plans that follow; some of which, from extending only to a few acres, may be thought too insignificant to admit of much nicety in regard to style; but when it is considered that this work is intended more for amateurs than for the improvement of artists, it will be at once perceived, that such illustration would be foreign to the uses of the work; for if artists themselves do not fully comprehend the nature and necessity of maintaining unity of style, what hopes can be entertained from delivering instructions to artisans or amateurs? The ground plans now to be described will be readily comprehended by them, and will, it is hoped, be found of some use.

Commencing with the lowest in the scale of extent,

PLATE VI.

is the first in order. It contains two designs for places of from three to six acres each, with kitchen garden, adapted for a family of six or eight persons, and paddock for a horse and cow.

In *Fig.* I. *a.* Is a public carriage road, which serves for this and another villa on the left.

b. Principal entrance to the house, under

c. A varandah, which leads to   *d.* The dining room.

e. Drawing room with the windows opening into

f. The Conservatory. *g.* Study.

h. Stairs down to the kitchen, and up to bed-chambers.

i. Lean-to office. *k.* Lean-to wash-house. *l.* Stable.

m. Cow-house. *n.* Chaise-house.

o. Poultry, &c. *p.* Piggery,

q. Fence of one rail or chain, which separates, the avenue to the garden from the paddock.

r. Fence of wire, to prevent sheep from entering the mowed ground, &c.

s. Gravel. *t.* Turf.

u. Clumps of strawberries, in which gooseberries, artichokes, asparagus; and other culinary shrubs and plants are introduced.

v. Dug work for flowers and tender shrubs.

w. Fruit wall and kitchen crops.

x. Fruit trees in kitchen garden.

y. Fruit shrubs in do. *z.* Edgings of strawberries.

It is to be observed, that the principal part of the trees, both in the pleasure ground and paddock, are fruit trees ; those of the forest species being chiefly a few of the more rare sorts, as sycamores, pines, evergreen oaks, &c. for variety ; and of the more hardy species, beech, elm, oak, lime, &c. for shelter.

Of the shrubs and flowers, a selection is used adapted to a perpetual garden, which of course ought to contain something for every season in the year.

Fig. 2. Pl. VI. Is a design in the geometrical or ancient style for a flat spot with no distant prospect.

a. The approach. *b.* Stables.

c. Pleasure ground, containing

d. A row of cut trees.

e. Dug, basket, and shell work, for flowers, and flowering shrubs.

f. A curiously clipt holly hedge.

o. A holly hedge for shelter, crossing the quarters of the garden.

p. Enriched or decorated ground, and parterres, placed near the house, and along

q. The garden margin of the water.

The disposition of the groups and thickets require no explanation.

PLATE VIII.

Is a design in the modern style for an irregular surface, with varied distant prospects, of fifty acres; such, for example, as are frequent in Surrey, Kent, and Hertfordshire.

The house is situated on the highest knoll, and the natural tendency of the lowest parts of the grounds is along the course of the water, which takes its rise from

a. A spring, which, before the lake was formed, assumed the character of a purling brook, as far as *b.* near the entrance lodge.

There are two approaches to this place, the one from the road, at *c.* and the other from *d.* The most agreeable distant scenery is seen over *e, f, g, h,* and *i.* The other parts, being less pleasing, are concealed by thicker plantations.

k. The kitchen garden, concealed by wood.

l. The family stables.

n. The farm buildings, for the few acres of corn grown in the fields, *m, m, m.*

n. These buildings, which appear pleasing features, seen from various points in the park.

o. The wire fence, which incloses some parterre decorations from the sheep, which alone graze the park.

p. Groups of flowers.

q. Flowering shrubs, aviary, and conservatory.

r. A vinery and peach house in the kitchen garden.

The walks, which make the circuit of the place, and the other component parts of this design, require no explanation.

PLATE IX.

Is a design for a flat surface of sixty acres, with no distant views that are agreeable; such, for example, as often occur in the western parts of Middlesex, and northern parts of Surrey. A circular sunk fence incloses the house, parterres, offices, and kitchen garden, which are arranged in Le Notre's style. The avenues and clumps require no explanation. On the whole, this is a most exact specimen, on a small scale, of the ancient style, and well calculated to produce an excellent effect in a dull level. A canal thirty or forty feet wide, with fountains, &c. running parallel to the sunk fence, is only wanting to complete the scene in the true geometric taste prevalent in Charles II.s' time.

PLATE X.

Is a design for one hundred acres, laid out in what has been called, by way of derision, Brown's manner. The surface is highest where the kitchen garden and surrounding shrubbery is placed, and lowest at the entrance lodge.

a. The water, conducted by art along a gentle slope; its natural course having been nearly parallel to the belt, at *b, c,* and *d.* It is raised to this situation (as at Wentworth castle) to

D

be better seen from the house, and to form what painters call an eye-trap in the landscape.

e. The clumps. *f*. Belt. *g*. Buildings in the belt.

h. Islands. *i*. Vistas in the belt.

k. Temple on an artificial knoll.

l. Cottage or shed, as an object from one of the buildings.

m. A sunk fence, enclosing the pleasure grounds, which surround the kitchen garden, and abound in clumps of various forms, but generally ovals or circles.

n. A greenhouse, heated by a pipe of hot air from the kitchen and other fires of the house.

o. The hot houses in the kitchen garden.

p. The court, or kitchen yard. *q*. The stable yard. *r*. Bridges.

Such places as these are very common, and may be considered as in a medium between the geometric and modern styles; the difference consisting in the character of the lines, which in the former are constantly straight, or distinct parts of regular figures, whereas in the latter they are constantly waving, or parts of serpentine lines. The former assumes the formality and distinction of ostentatious art; the latter affects the grace, ease, and beauty of nature. Both are characteristic of the age in which they were introduced. As affording variety in the general appearance of a country, grounds in Mr. Browns style, when not too obtrusive and destructive of general character, may sometimes be preserved, but they ought seldom to be created.

CHAP. III.

On the Formation and Arrangement of Kitchen Gardens; referring to Plates XI. XII. XIII. and XIV.

In laying out a villa, three principal considerations present themselves respecting the kitchen garden: first, its situation relatively to the mansion and other parts of the grounds; secondly, its exposure; and, thirdly, its formation.

1st, *Situation.* A kitchen garden ought to be near to, and on the same side of the house with the kitchen and the stables, for obvious reasons; and generally not far from the mansion, because if it contains hot houses and flowers, it is often resorted to in winter, as the most comfortable and agreeable scene for a morning walk. It must also be so situated as to be readily planted out; at least partially, both from the general prospect of the place, and the particular views from the house. A good soil, or one improvable, admitting of drainage, and affording water for horticultural purposes, are essential requisites.

2d, *Exposure.* A southern exposure, or one inclining to the east or west, are indispensable in gardens intended for early fruits or vegetables. Late gardens may have northern exposures; and general gardens, exposures to various aspects. In flats there is no choice. Whatever be the exposure, it will always be found requisite to possess shelter on three sides of a garden, especially the north. The south may generally be open, or partially sheltered at some distance from the walls, so as not to overshadow the garden in the winter months when the sun is low.

3d, *Formation.* This naturally includes extent, which depends upon the number of the family, and the season of the year in which they reside at the place. It also depends not a little on the skill of the gardener, and the scarcity or abundance of manure. A skilful manager with command of manure will grow more vegetables on a rood, than another with little manure will raise on an acre. In general, it may be remarked, that a garden, containing one acre within walls, will suffice for a family averaging twenty persons throughout the year. One rood will keep ten persons in common vegetables for a year, exclusive of wall fruits, and such salading as requires to be reared in hot beds. With regard to form, where no external circumstance or purpose in view indicates a particular shape, that of a parallelogram will be found the most generally useful, as affording the largest space of useful ground in the quarters, with the least quantity of useless angles or intersecting walks.

Where a kitchen garden includes the orchard, and is in part also a flower or ornamental garden, the form may be varied, and curve lines occasionally introduced to relieve the sameness of a square shape. This was done with great effect in the gardens laid out during the prevalency of the geometrical style of improvement. An example of a garden in this style is given in Plate XIV. which combines kitchen, fruit, flower, botanic, and exotic garden; is surrounded by a shrubbery; and which, by the great extent and variety of its walks, is well calculated for an interesting walk during the winter season.

(21)

PLATE XI.

Contains three designs for small gardens, in situations where external planting is deemed unnecessary, and where no use is made of the outside of the walls or boundary fences. Such cases occur constantly in places of a few acres in level situations near towns.

Fig. 1. Will answer for a rood or three quarters of an acre in extent, and suit a family consisting of six or eight persons.

a. The outer wall of brick. *b.* Elevations of do. *c.* Walk.

d. e. Section, shewing the relative height of the walls and espaliers, and the slope of the surface of the borders.

f. Inner border, with a row of gooseberries and an espalier rail; the border intended for flowers or salading.

g. Alley, separating the border from the quarters.

h. Quarters, for common kitchen crops.

i. Shifting glass frame, to ripen peaches or vines.

k. Wall border, for early or tender kitchen crops.

l. Box edgings to the walks.

Fig. 2. Is calculated for a plot of half an acre or upwards, and will serve a family of ten or twelve persons, with all the vegetables and fruits usually grown in gardens.

In this, all the fruit trees and shrubs are placed by themselves, in the quarters *a.* and *b.* in order to make the utmost of the ground, and to prevent inconvenience from the rounded shape of the two quarters devoted to fruit trees.

c. The borders of the walks, formed of strawberries a foot broad; the wall is brick, ten feet high on every side.

d. The forcinghouse, which has a tool house, fruit and seed room at one end, and a gardener's lodge at the other.

e. Borders of strawberries, two feet wide, to be used instead of alleys.

Fig. 3. Is a design for a garden, where the growth of fruit, and an agreeable lounge, are the principal objects. It may contain two thirds, or a whole acre.

a. The north walls are of pales ten feet high, as shewn in the elevation.

b. The south rail, six feet high, is of espalier work, to admit the sun to

c. c. The border. *d.* Are dwarf standards instead of espaliers.

e. Gooseberries.

f. Raspberry plantation, with standard fruit trees intermixed.

g. Currant plantations, with standards, &c.

h. Arbour, covered with hops or vines.

i. Box edgings. *k.* Alleys.

This forms a cheap and elegant garden for an estate held on lease: if the pales are of oak, or of any other timber well tarred and pitched, they will prove very warm in summer, from the dark colour absorbing the sun's rays; and they will last seventeen or twenty years.

PLATE XII.

Contains four designs adapted for particular situations.

Fig. 1. Is a plan for forming a garden, or rather for saving plots of ground for kitchen services out of plantations or shrubberies; it requires hardly any explanation.

a. Are the alleys. *b.* Water.

c. A range of pits for vines, peaches, melons, &c.

This plan answers remarkably well when wall-fruit is dispensed with, and where the seat or villa is chiefly resorted to in summer, when the dry walks, and comfort of a walled garden, are less an object. In short, it is the cheapest way of raising common vegetables on a small place, consistently with the object of preserving the appearance of plantation and extent.

Fig. 2. Is adapted to a plot of irregular shape, and combines a shrubbery with a kitchen garden. It may be of any size, according to the wants of the family and the season of their residence, &c.

a. Entrance. *b.* Melon pits and hot beds.

c. Fruit trees and shrubs.

d. Centre walk, with rows of espaliers and gooseberries on each side.

e. Vine, pine, and peach houses.

f. Shed and gardener's lodge.

g. Water raised by an engine to a cistern on the top of the shed, whence pipes are conducted to each house, so as to admit their being watered by screwing leather tubes to them at pleasure, in the manner of fire engines.

h. Covered seat.

i. Forest trees for shelter, the sorts diminishing in size as they approach the garden walk, where shrubs and flowers only are used.

This forms a very beautiful garden, and is adapted for irregular hollows, chalk, gravel, or stone pits, dingles, or rocky situations.

Fig. 3. This design is calculated for the centre of a wood, or for any situation where the shape may be desirable. In the centre of a high wood, it affords more sun and shelter than any other form.

a. Glass house in the centre.

b. Zig-zag pales, or wooden walls, placed in that position for strength, and for obtaining in a short distance a considerable length of wall.

(24)

c. Outer border of fruit trees and shrubs, bounded by a clipt holly hedge.

d. Inner borders of dwarf standards and fruit shrubs.

Fig. 4. Is calculated for a narrow situation running north and south. It is divided by cross walls for shelter, and to obtain extent of south walling, in proportion to the east and west walls. This form is adapted to one, two, and three acres.

a. Principal entrance. *b.* Melon ground.

c. Vine, pine, peach, and house for forcing cherries, &c.

d. Sheds, gardener's lodge, and mushroom house, with cistern over.

e. Sheds for furnaces to *f.* The hot walls.

g. Borders of gooseberries and espaliers.

h. Borders of dwarf standards and fruit shrubs.

PLATE XIII.

Exhibits a design for a garden, to contain from two to four acres within the outer walk. It is surrounded by a shrubbery and wood for shelter (*a.*), and the melon ground and yard for compost heaps, &c. (*b.*); is placed in a recess, in a gently rising slope, behind the hot houses (*c.*)

The principal part of the standard fruit trees are planted in the shrubbery, (a mode adopted with great success by the late Mr. Forsyth, in the royal gardens, Kensington); and in the borders, dwarf trees and gooseberries are preferred to espaliers, which occasion much more trouble, are not more sure of bearing, nor more productive in favourable seasons.

In other respects it requires no explanation. This plan was generally adopted by the late worthy Mr. Nicol, designer of gardens, near Edinburgh, and is particularly adapted to a cold country.

PLATE XIV.

Is a design, in the magnificent taste of the old French school of improvement. It combines grandeur, variety, and utility, by its extent, marked form, the elegance of the glass houses, &c. It contains,

1. A surrounding shrubbery, planted with every common sort of tree, shrub, standard fruit tree, and flowering plant. See *n.* in the plan.

2. A range of glass houses, containing culinary exotics, and forcing houses of every description, in the divisions *d.* and *f.* and of botanic or shewy exotics in the divisions *e.* and *g.*

3. An orchard of standard fruit trees, *o.*

4. Quarters and borders for culinary vegetables, at *p. l.* and *m.* and

5. A complete botanic arrangement, at *h. h.*

a. Is the principal entrance.

b. Circles of evergreen shrubs and trees with flowers, and fruit trees, and on the walk on each side, a seat of a curved form, six or eight feet in length.

c. Basin and fountain, from whence the water may be forced by engines to cisterns on the tops of the hot houses, in order to irrigate them and the walls and quarters of the garden. This is effected by means of conducting tubes to screw on and off the stationary cocks at pleasure, in the manner of fire engines.

i. Obelisk, clock, and dial.

k. Borders of espalier and gooseberries.

l. Border and hot wall.

q. Furnace sheds, and lodge for gardeners.

Such a garden is the most interesting that can be formed at a town villa, or a winter or spring residence in the country.

E

CHAP IV.

On laying out Parterres and Flower Gardens; referring to Plates XV. XVI. and XVII.

Of these there are two kinds; first, such as are small and may be comprehended at one view; and, secondly, such as are of considerable size, containing forest trees.

A symmetrical form is best adapted to the former, and an irregular shape to the latter; both classes may be treated together, under the heads of *Relative situation, character, and composition* or *materials.*

1. *Relative situation.* It is obvious that flower gardens should be near the house, since the beauties of flowers are of a minute and changeable nature; to be enjoyed therefore, they must be frequently examined, which is not likely to be the case, where they are placed in less frequented parts of the grounds: as works of art, they are also with propriety placed near what is in every place the centre of art and refinement,—the mansion. Hence they are generally formed on the lawn, either in characters of regular outline and symmetry, as connected with Gothic or ancient architecture; or in irregular groups and compartments, as connected with mansions in the modern taste. Occasionally they are introduced in kitchen gardens, and in different parts of a general tract of ornamented ground, and there form various scenes of show or curiosity. Where a walk is wanted through a lawn, in a flat situation, it cannot be made interesting in any manner so easily, as by a chain of curious gardens

and parterres in succession, with intervals of grove, wood, avenue thicket, or open lawn.

2. *Character.* These are various. The modern style, as already mentioned, is a collection of irregular groups or masses, placed about the house as a 'medium, uniting it with the open lawn. The ancient geometric style, in place of irregular groups, employed symmetrical f orms; in France, adding statues and fountains; in Holland, cut trees and grassy slopes; and in Italy, stone walls, walled terraces, and flights of steps. In some situations, these characteristics of parterres may with propriety be added to, or used instead of the modern sort, especially in flat situations, such as are enclosed by high walls in towns, or where the principal building or object is in a style of architecture which will not render these appendages incongruous.

There are other characters of gardens, such as the Chinese, which are not widely different from the modern; the Indian, which consist chiefly in straight walks under shade, in squares of grass, &c.; the Turkish, which abound in shady retreats, boudoirs of roses and aromatic herbs; and the Spanish, which are distinguished by trellis work and fountains: but these gardens not being generally adapted to this climate, it has been deemed preferable to omit them, though from contemplating the whole, and selecting what is beautiful, or suitable in each, a style of decoration for the immediate vicinity of m ansions might be composed, greatly preferable to any thing now in use. Such a style of decoration, however, would be chiefly applicable to places of considerable extent; and therefore does not come within the limited plan of the present publication.

3. *Composition* or *Materials.* Much might be written on this subject; since, on the plants employed, much more than the

form of the grounds or walks, depends the effect or beauty of
the parterre. The prevailing error consists in two extremes:
crowding them with all sorts of trees and plants at random, or
filling them entirely with rare species, which will ever want one
principal source of beauty, *health.* Sickliness in the plants, and
lumpish, clumsy outlines in the dug work, may truly be said
to characterize too many of even the best parterres in this
country.

Another error is the neglect of distinguishing between
parterres for the whole year, and those for particular seasons;
to have the former in perfection, it is essentially necessary to
keep the greater number of the plants in pots, in order to re-
move them when done flowering and introduce others. In a
complete garden, there ought to be departments or parterres
for every month in the year. In all others, every attention
ought to be paid to introduce only appropriate plants and
shrubs.

Lawn, earth, shells, curious rock work, sand, flints, &c. are
employed in French parterres; together with fountains, basins,
statues, clipt shrubs, trellis work, &c. Ample information on
this subject may be found in Le Blond's Theory and Practice
of Gardening.

PLATE XV.

This plate contains three parterres in the common English
style, composed chiefly of grass, gravel, and dug work. The
grass is kept constantly mown, the gravel rolled smooth, the dug
work somewhat rounded and raised above the grass, from which
it is distinctly separated by repeatedly paring the turf.

(29)

The dug compartments may be surrounded with basket work, or left naked, as taste or economy may direct.

Fig. 1. Is in the commonest form of British flower gardens.

a. Gravel walks. *b.* Dug borders. *c.* Turf.

d. Cypress trees. *e.* Water, fountain, obelisk, &c.

f. Shrubbery.

Figs. 2. and 3. Require no explanation, except that both of them are supposed to be surrounded by a thick plantation of holly, kept shorn on the side next the parterres.

PLATE XVI.

Fig. 1. Is a design in the flowery style of the French, or what they call a parterre of embroidery. It is composed of gravel, shells, turf, earth, water, clipt trees, basket work, and flowers placed in pots; the pots placed in the earth, to be removed and replaced by others at pleasure.

a. Gravel. *b.* Turf. *c.* Dug work. *d.* Shells.

e. Baskets. *f.* Clipt trees and shrubs.

g. Statue and basin, with fountain.

h. Hedge of yew tree, cut into niches or colonnades, and surmounted with equestrian statues in yew.

i. Seats.

These works in yew, are first formed in wire work, and the yew, or other hedge plants, trained within the mould thus formed, their extremities being clipt off as they obtrude beyond the form which they are destined to assume.

Fig. 2. Is a design in the German and Scotch style, calculated for dug work, edged by flowers and gravel, with some turf, a basin, and fountain.

a. Gravel. *b.* Edging of box, thrift, daisy, &c.

c. Turf. *d.* Seats. *e.* Avenues of limes. *f.* Shrubbery.

Fig. 3. Is a design in the modern English style, with additions in the French manner. It is composed of gravel, turf, dug groups, basket work, borders, and patches, with a conservatory or orangery, and a covered walk of trellis work.

a. Conservatory and aviary.

b. Compartments of basket work. *c.* Grass.

d. Earth or dug work.

e. Cones, columns, statues of wire for creepers, trellis work, on which roses are trained, &c. &c.

f. Covered walks and seats. *g.* Shrubbery.

h. Creepers, ferns, &c. running wild on the lawn.

i. Open seats. *k.* Sheltered or covered seats.

PLATE XVII.

Is a design for a botanical arrangement, intended to comprise a complete collection of the vegetables growing in this country, arranged agreeably to the *Systema Naturæ* of Lin_næus; the glass houses in the centre contain the exotics.

a. The stove plants. *b.* The dry stove.

c. Those of the green house.

Class 1. Order 1. begins adjoining the glass houses, and is denoted thus, 1|1. An irregular patch is allotted to each class and order, according in size with the number of hardy trees and plants belonging to [each, which are to be had in the nurseries or botanic gardens of this country. The glades between the classes and orders are of smooth turf, blending with the trees and plants, and to be diminished as it may be requisite to enlarge the groups for the introduction of new species.

This garden is surrounded by a shrubbery, chiefly of evergreens, for shelter, intermixed with fruit trees, for show in spring. There are also open glades of lawn, and covered seats, in the usual manner.

CHAP. V.

On the Formation of Groves, Woods, Labyrinths, Shrubberies, Plantations, Borders, &c.; referring to Plate XVIII.

These form essential parts of every country seat; the hints submitted, are therefore extended in proportion to the importance of the subject.

1. *Groves.* A grove may be defined a collection of trees, on a smooth surface without undergrowth, planted at such a distance from each other as to admit of their attaining considerable magnitude. Thus an orchard may be designated a grove of fruit trees, &c. When the trees used are all of the same species, the effect is the most complete: a grove of lime or ash trees is among the most elegant and agreeable in summer; of oaks, chesnuts, or pines, the most grand. A grove may either be without walks, or laid out in avenues and recesses in the geometric taste, or a natural road may pass through it in the modern manner.

2. *Woods.* A wood differs only from a grove in having undergrowth: in every other respect they are alike.

It is proper to observe that formal groves, or woods, are now seldom introduced in a detached form and character, but come in naturally as component parts of the forest or woody scenery of a large place. In the geometrical style, however, they claim a conspicuous part, for which reason is given the example, *Fig.* I. Pl. XVIII. which will answer equally well for a grove or a wood, in a flat or not very uneven tract of eight or ten acres or upwards.

3. *Labyrinths,* partaking of the conceits of the age in which they were produced, are mere puzzles for children. They are amusing and appropriate in a residence laid out in the ancient taste, and therefore an example is here introduced, see Pl. XVIII. *Fig.* 2.

4. *Shrubberies, Plantations,* and *Borders.* These are common to every place, and require therefore to be particularly treated of. Shrubberies are plantations of ornamental trees, flowering shrubs, and plants, with walks through them : the trees and shrubs arranged according to their heights, having a mixture of flowers and shrubs rising in gradation from the edge of the walk.

Plantations differ from shrubberies in not containing ornamental shrubs or flowers.

Borders are dug strips, of a few feet broad, in gardens or pleasure grounds, and are planted with fruit trees and flowers, or ornamental shrubs and flowering plants.

Sir Wm. Chambers. Mr. Price, and others, have questioned the propriety of the customary arrangement of trees, shrubs, and plants, in these subjects of gardening, alleging the indiscriminate mixture of many different species to be unnatural, and productive neither of character nor beauty. It is presumed that the rules for a right practice in these matters, as well as in planting in general, will be given with most effect by extracts from their works.

" In their plantations, the Chinese artists do not, as is the
" practice of some European gardeners, plant indiscriminately
" every thing that comes in their way ; nor do they ignorantly
" imagine, that the whole perfection of plantations, consists in
" the variety of trees and shrubs of which they are composed :
" on the contrary, their practice is guided by many rules,

" founded on reason and long observation, from which they
" seldom, if ever deviate.

" This excessive variety in plantations, the Chinese artists
" severely blame; observing that a great diversity of colours,
" foliage, and direction of branches, must create confusion, and
" destroy all the masses upon which effect and grandeur depend :
" they observe, too, that it is unnatural; for as in nature most
" plants sow their own seeds, whole forests are generally com-
" posed of the same sort of trees. They admit, however, of a
" moderate variety, but are by no means promiscuous in the
" choice of their plants; attending with great care to the colour,
" form, and foliage of each; and only mixing together such as
" harmonize and assemble agreably.

" They observe that some trees are only proper for thickets ;
" others only fit to be employed singly; and others equally
" adapted to both these situations. The mountain cedar, the
" spruce and silver firs, and all others whose branches have a
" horizontal direction, they hold improper for thickets ; because
" they indent into each other, and likewise cut disagreeably upon
" the plants which back them. They never mix these horizontal
" branched trees with the cypress, the oriental arbor vitæ, the
" bamboo, and other upright ones ; nor with the larix, the weeping
" willow, the birch, the laburnum, or any of a pendant nature ;
" observing, that the intersection of their branches forms a very
" unpicturesque kind of network : neither do they employ
" together the catalpha and the acacia, the yew and the willow,
" the plane and the sumach, nor any of such heterogeneous sorts ;
" but, on the contrary, they assemble in their large woods the
" oak, the elm, the beech, the tulip, the sycamore, maple, and
" plane, the Indian chesnut, the tong-shu, and the western
" walnut, the arbeal, the lime, and all whose luxuriant foliages

F

" hide the direction of their branches, and growing in globular
" masses, assemble well together; forming, by the harmonious
" combination of their tints, one grand group of rich verdure.

" In their smaller plantations, they employ trees of a smaller
" growth, but of the same concordant sorts; bordering them with
" Persian lilacs, gelder roses, seringas, coronillas or sennas of
" various sorts, flowering rasberries, yellow jessamine, hyperi-
" cum or St. John's wort, the speræa frutex, altheas, roses, and
" other flowering shrubs peculiar to China.

" In their shrubberies they follow, as much as possible, the
" same rules; observing, farther, to plant in some of them all
" such shrubs as flourish at one time; and in some, such as suc-
" ceed each other: of which different methods, the first is much
" the most brilliant; but its duration is short, and the appear-
" ance of the shrubbery is generally shabby as soon as the bloom
" is off; they therefore seldom use it, but for scenes that are to
" be enjoyed at certain periods, preferring the last, on other oc-
" casions, as being of long duration, and less unpleasing after
" the flowers are gone.

" The Chinese gardeners do not scatter their flowers indiscrimi-
" nately about their borders, as is usual in some parts of Europe,
" but dispose them with great circumspection; and, if I may be
" allowed the expression, paint their way very artfully along the
" skirts of the plantations, or other places where flowers are to
" be introduced. They reject all that are of a straggling growth,
" of harsh colours, and poor foliage; choosing only such as are of
" some duration, grow either large or in clusters, are of beautiful
" forms, well leaved, and of tints that harmonize with the greens
" that surround them. They avoid all sudden transitions, both
" with regard to dimension and colour; rising gradually from the
" smallest flowers to holly oaks, p æonies, sun-flowers, carnation,

" poppies, and others of the boldest growth ; and varying their
" tints, by easy gradations, from white, straw colour, purple, and
" incarnate, to the deepest blues, and most brilliant crimsons and
" scarlets. They frequently blend several roots together, whose
" leaves and flowers unite and compose one rich harmonious
" mass ; such as the white and purple candituff, larkspurs, and
" mallows of various colours, double poppies, lupins, primroses,
" pinks and carnations, with many more of which the forms and
" colours accord with each other; and the same method they use
" with flowering shrubs; blending white, red, and variegated
" roses together; purple and white lilacs; yellow and white
" jessamine; altheas of various sorts; and as many others as they
" can with any propriety unite. By these mixtures they increase
" considerably the variety and beauty of their compositions.

" In their large plantations, the flowers generally grow in the
" natural ground ; but in flower gardens, and all other parts that
" are highly kept, they are in pots, buried in the ground ; which,
" as fast as the bloom goes off, are removed, and others are
" brought to supply their places ; so that there is a constant
" succession for almost every month in the year, and the flowers
" are never seen, but in the height of their beauty." Sir William
" Chambers on Oriental Gardening, page 87.

" Variety," Mr. Price observes, " of which the true end is to re-
" lieve the eye, not to perplex it, does not consist in the diversity
" of separate objects, but in that of their effects when combined
" together, in diversity of composition, and of character. Many
" think, however, they have obtained that grand object, when
" they have exhibited in one body all the hard names of the
" Linnæan system: but when as many different plants as can well
" be got together, are exhibited in every shrubbery, or in every
" plantation, the result is a sameness of a different kind, but not

" less truly a sameness, than would arise from there being no
" diversity at all; for there is no having variety of character,
" without a certain distinctness, without certain marked fea-
" tures on which the eye can dwell.

" In forests and woody commons, we sometimes come from
" a part where hollies had chiefly prevailed, to another where
" junipers or yews are the principal evergreens; and where,
" perhaps, there is the same sort of change in the deciduous
" underwood. This strikes us with a new impression; but mix
" them equally together in all parts, and diversity becomes
" a source of monotony.

" One great cause of the superior variety and richness of un-
" improved parks and forests, when compared with lawns and
" dressed grounds, and of their being so much more admired by
" painters, is, that the trees and groups are seldom totally alone
" and unconnected; that they seldom exhibit either of those two
" principal defects in the composition of landscapes. the opposite
" extremes of being too crowded or too scattered; whereas the
" clump is a most unhappy union of them both: it is scattered
" in respect to the general composition, and close and lumpish
" when considered by itself. Single trees, when they stand alone
" and are round-headed, have some tendency towards the defects
" of the clump; and it is worthy of remark, that in the Liber
" Veritatis of Claude, consisting of nearly two hundred drawings,
" there are not, I believe, more than three single trees. This is
" one strong proof, which the works of other painters would
" fully confirm, that those who most studied the effect of visible
" objects, attended infinitely less to their distinct individual
" forms, than to their grouping and connection." Price's
Essays, vol. I. p. 286.

PLATE XVIII.

Contains a design for a grove, a labyrinth, and one for laying out a public square.

Fig. 1. Is a grove laid out in the geometric taste.

a. Principal entrance. *b.* Lodge and prospect tower.

c. Basin with fountains; seven jets d'eau, being seen at once from the tower, and from the points, *a. b. d. e. f. g. h.* and *i.*

Such a grove may occupy from five to fifty acres.

Fig. 2. Is a design for a labyrinth, to extend over three or four acres; or if planted with yew, it may be confined to one acre, or even to a rood.

a. Entrance.

b. Basin and fountain in the centre, with seats, &c.

c. Wood with under-growth of box, yew, or privet and thorn, kept clipt on the sides.

Fig. 3. Is a design for laying out a public square.

a. Outer border of trees and evergreens, under-growth.

b. Outer walk, for winter or wet weather, being exposed to the air and sun;—this walk is on a level with the street.

c. Slope to the inner walk.

d. Inner walk, or avenue two feet lower than the outer one, and shaded with lime trees.

e. Walks on the same level, running to the centre.

f. Column and colossal statue in the centre, with covered seats.

g. Raised bank of enriched plantation or shrubbery, making those walks towards the centre a complete umbrageous promenade. Seats are placed on the sides of the walks.

h. Open seats in different parts of the square.

i. Clumps of evergreens and flowers.

k. Single trees with creepers, and the thorn and crabs bearing misletoe, &c.

CHAP. VI.

On the construction of Hot houses, Glass varandahs, Wall frames, Hot beds, Pits, Hot walls, Conservatories, Espaliers, &c.

Hot houses. In order to produce a complete artificial climate at the least expence, a moderate sized house is preferable to either extreme; from seventy to ninety feet of air is a proper quantity for being heated by one fire. Magnitude can only be desirable in green houses or conservatories, and in them is perfectly admissible, as the aid of fire is required only for the most severe weather.

In the construction of every description of hot houses, cast iron rafters, pillars, and standards with copper sashes, doors, and lights, are much to be preferred to wood. The difference in expence at first is but trifling, while the durability of the house, its superiority for the purpose of forcing, or protecting exotics by admitting more light, is unquestionable. The supposed danger from lightning is in a great measure done away by inserting the ends of some of the upwright rafters, or of rods attached to them, three or four feet in the earth.

The principal expence of these elegant and luxurious appendages to a garden is the glass. In ornamental houses, in parterres, or adjoining drawing rooms, large squares of glass are desirable; but in common forcing houses in kitchen gardens, they ought to be of a small size. Copper sashes, from the narrowness of the astragals, are particularly adapted for this purpose, and by allowing the use of a smaller sized pane, by not twisting and casting like wood, save in expence of glass much more than their extra cost.

"The price of the superficial foot of glass, (observes Mr.
" Nicol, in 1805), varying according to the size of the squares, it
" is of importance not to make these too large; for instance, a
" square which is twelve inches on the side, and which contains
" just a foot of glass, is sold at tenpence; (I speak of third
" crown); whereas two squares, eight and a half by eight and a
" half inches each, and which contain the same quantity to a
" mere fraction, is sold at sixpence halfpenny. So that the
" smaller the square, the cheaper is the superficial foot of glass ;
" and this is occasioned by the small squares being cut from the
" broke or waste of the large ones, which, if the manufacturer
" has no market for, he is under the necessity of remelting." See
Nicol's Forcing Gardener, p. 237.

The best mode of constructing flues, appears to be that of forming the smoke chamber of cast iron, and imbedding or surrounding it with brick work. The former material conducts the heat, while the latter absorbs it, and gives it out slowly to the atmosphere of the house as wanted. It must be confessed, however, that this mode is too expensive for general use; and therefore, for ordinary cases, the usual mode by brick sides and tyle covers is preferable.

The furnace, with double doors, of the construction recommended by Count Rumford, is perhaps, for general purposes, as good as any: at all events, it is less intricate and troublesome to ordinary labourers, than the newer, and more complete plans of Stewart, Loudon, and some others. An inner curtain has been used successfully at several places. It is probable, however, that an outer one of sail cloth would effect nearly the same purpose, with less inconvenience and trouble, in rolling up and letting down. In severe climates, and where winter forcing is much in use, they will be found a great advantage. In pine stoves they need never be used, as pines will endure a much greater degree of cold without injury, than most gardeners have any idea of. This every gentleman, acquainted with their culture abroad, and the climates in the East Indies, will readily allow. The author has seen them, in some parts of this country, grown in a superior style, without bottom heat; and in a temperature, at an average, ten degrees lower than that commonly deemed proper for pines.

Steam; dung; a stream of hot water from breweries, and distilleries; sun heat, as in Dr. Anderson's hot house; and various other contrivances, have been adopted for heating glass houses; but to enter minutely into their different merits would exceed the limits of this work, in which it is intended to give an example or two, on a moderate scale and simple plan, adapted to villas of moderate size, and suited to the capacity of ordinary gardeners. A simple plan, in which there is little danger of the workmen going wrong in the construction, and of the gardener erring in the management, is better suited for general utility, than more brilliant, ingenious, and really superior schemes, that in clever hands would facilitate the objects in view, and save expence.

PLATE XIX.

Fig. 1. Is a range of houses on a small scale for vines, pines, and peaches, and for preserving a few green-house and hot-house plants.

a. Peach-house. The trees trained on a wire trellis, two feet from the glass, with a stage behind for green-house plants. These plants, as soon as forced into blossom, or to a luxuriant state of growth, may be removed into the drawing room.

b. Pinery and exotics. The pines are planted in a sloping bed of earth, raised within five feet of the glass: no bottom heat is applied, as being unnatural, and from the experience of some gardeners, unnecessary.

The only path in this house is along the top of the flue, in front, three feet wide. An arch is thrown over this flue at both ends of the house, to support the earth of the pit or shed, and admit the heat of the flue to the air of the house.

c. The vinery ; the vines trained like the peaches, with a stage for forcing strawberries, french beans, &c. behind.

Fig. 2. *d.* Fire-places, and coal-sheds.

e. Sheds for pots, earth, &c.

f. Smoke flues.

Fig. 3. Is a plan suited to the same elevation, and calculated for being heated by stable dung thrown into the pits, *a. a.* and removed gradually as the violence of fermentation subsides. The heat ascends through the brick arch thrown over these pits, and is absorbed by the mass of rubble work, or brick-bats, flints, &c. *b. b.* around them. These masses of stones or bricks serve as reservoirs of heat, when the dung is changed, or when the fermentation is less brisk, &c. Hot-

G

houses on this principle may be erected wherever four or six horses are kept, or where the farm yard adjoins the garden or the stables.

The hot-houses in Plate VII. *Fig.* 2. are constructed and heated on this principle.

Glass varandahs. These are in many respects preferable to those of canvas, slating, or boards, as admitting more light to apartments in winter, and affording an opportunity of growing excellent grapes, or other fruits, or flowering creepers, under them in summer. But glass varandahs, green-houses, and conservatories, against houses, have a vulgar hot-bed-like appearance, when executed in the common mode. A plan for varying this, by a sort of light parapet, on which to train creepers, is submitted in *Fig.* 4. of this Plate, which contains five varieties, requiring no farther explanation than what is shewn in the section, *Fig.* 5.

Wall frames. One of the best modes of procuring large high-flavoured fruit, is by simply applying glass frames against the trees, (whether peaches or vines), on a common wall. The fruit will be about a fortnight earlier than if unprotected. The sashes must be occasionally removed to admit the rain and dews, and a vacuity left between every sixth or tenth sash, to admit air. One advantage attending this mode of forcing is, that its success is very little, if at all dependent on the skill or attention of the gardener.

In the section, *Fig.* 6. *a. a.* Is the frame to be placed against the wall.

b. The wall against which the frame is placed.

c. The supports of oak, charred fir, or (which is much to be preferred) cast iron, driven into the ground, one between every two sashes, to support the corners of each.

Conservatories. Pl. XX. is a design for a conservatory of considerable size, and supposed to be placed in the centre of such a flower garden as *Fig.* 1. Pl. XV. and approached under a glass or trellis varandah. Such approaches have the double effect of being cool and shady in summer, and warm and dry in winter, and are besides capable of yielding much fruit. Should glass be thought too expensive, it might be formed wholly of trellis or canvas work.

The canal in the centre of the conservatory may contain fountains, fish, exotics, and aquatics, and grapes and creepers may be planted to train up the rafters and round the supporting pillars.

Houses of this sort, on a smaller scale, may be contrived to have the glass taken off in June, and the plants exposed to the air, and turfed round in the manner of the orangery at Nuneham. The glass may then be used as wall frames for maturing fruit on the walls, or for growing melons, &c.

Hot-beds. ~~Dung-beds ought~~ wholly to be excluded from gardens, as there is not a more ruinous mode of using manure. Twelve two-horse loads of fresh stable dung, that would manure an acre, are required for an ordinary three-light frame; it remains under this frame for nine months, in order to grow half a dozen melons, (which might be as well raised by fire heat), and when removed will not manure a rood. Pits heated by fire, will answer every purpose of these dung-beds, and considering the great advantages that would occur to agriculture, from the manure thus saved, it is surely time they were substituted in their room.

Copper sashes, and cast iron frames, which take asunder so as to be perfectly portable, are much to be preferred to the usual wooden ones, which soon rot, and are continually warping, so as to break the glass.

Espalier rails. The chief advantage of using these in gardens, is that more room is obtained on the borders for vegetables. They ought always to be constructed of cast iron, and fixed in stones sunk and made fast in the ground. The Author is now constructing a serpentine espalier rail in cast iron, which when erected will be one of the most complete things of the kind in England. The advantages of a serpentine form are, that it breaks the force of the wind, when parallel to the rail.

Hot-walls. The chief disadvantage attending the use of flued walls is, that the least excess of fire is apt to make the blossom, and sometimes even the fruit and leaves drop off, from that part of the tree trained against the flues. This being more frequently the case with the two first courses of the flue, attempts have been made to remedy the evil by using wider bricks in the front of that part of the wall. It is doubtful, however, whether this does not rather increase it than otherwise, since a larger mass of materials must necessarily retain a greater quantity of heat. The only effectual mode is to apply a wire or wooden trellis to the wall, commencing at the surface of the ground, projecting an inch or two, and reaching half the height of the wall, inclining towards it till it there touches the surface and is discontinued. The top part never being so overheated as to endanger the blossoms, requires no trellis. Another advantage of this trellis is, that by throwing the trees out of the perpendicular, greater benefit is derived from dews and summer showers. The only use of hot-walls is to counteract frosts in spring, during the blossom of the trees; and in autumn to facilitate the ripening of wood and fruit; they ought seldom to be used for the purposes of forcing, even when canvas awnings for shelter in severe weather are adopted : when this is done, the consequence is too frequently a total want of success.

Fig. 7. Pl. XIX. is a specimen of the basket work alluded to in Chapters I. and II.

a. The stakes or props on which it rests, placed three or four feet asunder.

b. A section of one side of the basket.

If these baskets or flower-frames are made of wood, well painted, and carefully removed and placed under cover in winter, they will last from ten to fifteen years; if of iron, of course they may be cast to any pattern, and will endure for ever.

French parterres, in which this sort of ornament is introduced, have a most superb effect; even common English flower-gardens are greatly enriched by them, as at Donnington, Blenheim, and Dalkeith.

Fig. 8. and 9. Are the elevation and plan of a house, with a green-house and glass varandah attached, and varied by a parapet in the manner before described.

a. Is the green-house, communicating with

b. The library.

c. The fire-place, for heating both the library and green-house.

d. Holes in the pavement for planting vines, to be trained up the wall and down the glass varandah; the wall behind being heated by the kitchen and scullery flues, which are carried slanting across it. A green-house and varandah somewhat in this manner, may be seen at the elegant villa of T. S. Barber, Esq. at Shepherd's Bush, near London; the whole of which indeed is most tastefully and economically arranged, from the proprietor's own designs.

CHAP. VII.

Lists of Trees and Plants, arranged so as to facilitate the choice of Species, adapted to particular situations in Orchards and Villa Grounds.

Of these lists it may be observed generally, that they only extend to such sorts as are to be obtained at any nursery. Whatever may be the beauty or botanical merits of rarer species, those here enumerated will ever form the principal features in the gardens and plantations of this climate.

LIST THE FIRST.—FOREST TREES AND SHRUBS.

The following list contains all the common forest trees and shrubs, *arranged according to their general time of flowering.* In each month the trees are placed first, and generally commencing with the tallest species, the next tallest follows, and so on through the month, ending with the shrubs which have the most diminutive growth. The heights in feet must be considered as very indefinite, trees varying in height according to soil and situation; but it was deemed better to state something in a decided way, in order to approximate to correctness of idea relatively. Thus in March, the larch is stated as a tree of sixty feet, and the white poplar of eighty; often they will be found growing together of nearly the same height; but the intention of the numerical distinction is to shew, that of a hundred full-grown larches, more will be found of sixty feet, than of fifty or seventy, and the same of the white poplar and of all the rest.

FOREST TREES AND SHRUBS.

JANUARY.

Linnean Names.	English Names.	Colour of the Blossom.	Height and Character.
1 Hydrangea hortensis	Changeable Hydrangea	Mixed	Shrub
2 Ruscus aculeatus	Prickly Butcher's-broom	Mixed	Shrub

FEBRUARY.

1 Taxus baccata	Common Yew Tree	Mixed	Low Tree
2 —— nucifera	Nut-bearing Yew Tree	Mixed	Low Tree

MARCH.

1 Pinus larix	Larch Fir	Mixed	Tree 60 F.
2 Populus alba	Great white Poplar	Mixed	Tree 80 F.
3 —— nigra	Black Poplar	Mixed	Do.
4 —— angulata	Angular Poplar	Mixed	Do.
5 —— tremula	Trembling Poplar	Mixed	Tree 50 F.
6 Corylus avelana	Common Hazel-Nut Tree	Mixed	Shrub
7 Atragene Austriaca	Austrian Atragene	Blue	Climber
8 Rhododendron Dauricum	Dauric Rosebay	Mixed	Shrub
9 Genista Lusitanica	Portugal Genista	Yellow	Shrub
10 Buxus sempervirens	Common Box Tree	Mixed	Low Shrub
11 Ledum buxifolium	Box-leaved Ledum	Mixed	Very low Shrub

APRIL.

1 Pinus rubra	Red Spruce Fir	Mixed	Tree 70 F.
2 —— abies	Norway Spruce	Mixed	Do.
3 —— strobus	Weymouth Pine	Mixed	Do.
4 Quercus robur	Common Oak Tree	Mixed	Do.
5 Fagus sylvatica	Common Beech Tree	Mixed	Tree 60 F.
6 Platanus orientalis	Oriental Plane Tree	Mixed	Tree 50 F.
7 Juglans regia	Common Walnut Tree	White	Tree 60 F.
8 Prunus padus	Bird Cherry Tree	White, showy	Tree 30 F.
9 Robinea spinosa	Thorny Robinea, or Acacia	White, showy	Tree 30 F.
10 Syringa vulgaris	Common Lilac	Purple and white	Shrub
11 —— Chinensis	Chinese Lilac	Purple	Shrub
12 —— Persica	Persian Lilac	Light blue	Low Shrub
13 Arbutus andrachni	Eastern Strawberry Tree	White	Shrub
14 Magnolia purpurea	Purple Magnolia	Purple	Do.

Linnean Names.	English Names.	Colour of the Blossom.	Height and Character.
15 Daphne Pontica	Two-flowered Daphne	Pale yellow	Shrub
16 Vaccinium virgatum	Twiggy Whort	Pale yellow	Do.
17 Ruscus hypoglossum	Double-leaved B. Broom	Mixed	Do.
18 Erica herbacea	Early Dwarf Heath	White and blue	Do.

MAY.

1 Pinus pinea	Stone Pine Fir	Mixed	Tree 40 F.
2 —— cedrus	Cedar of Lebanon	Mixed	Tree 30 F.
3 —— balsamea	Balm of Gilead Fir Tree	Mixed	Tree 60 F.
4 —— Canadensis	Hemlock Spruce	Mixed	Tree 20 F.
5 —— nigra	Black Spruce	Mixed	Tree 50 F.
6 Acer pseudo-platanus	Sycamore Tree	Mixed	Tree 40 F.
7 —— Tartaricum	Tartarian Maple	Mixed	Tree 30 F.
8 —— rubrum	Scarlet Maple	Mixed	Tree 30 F.
9 Carpinus betulus	Common Hornbeam Tree	Mixed	Tree 50 F.
10 Salisburia Adiantifolia	Maiden-Hair leaved Tree	Mixed	Shrub
11 Cratægus torminalis	Wild Service Tree	Cream-coloured	Low Tree
12 ———— oxyacantha	White Thorn	White	Do.
13 ———— azarolus	Azarole Thorn	White	Do.
14 ———— crus galli	Cock-spur Thorn	White	Do.
15 ———— odoratissima	Sweet-scented Thorn	White and Scarlet	Do.
16 Quercus ilex	Evergreen Oak Tree	Mixed	Tree 40 F.
17 —— coccinea	Scarlet Oak Tree	Mixed	Tree 30 F.
18 Thuja occidentalis	American Arbor Vitæ	Mixed	Shrub
19 —— orientalis	China Arbor Vitæ	Mixed	Shrub
20 Cytisus laburnum	Laburnum	Yellow	Low Tree
21 Mespilus pyracantha	Evergreen Thorn	Purple	Fruit Shrub
22 Viburnum opulus	Gelder Rose	White	Shrub
23 ———— lantanoides	Large flowering Viburnum	White	Shrub
24 Prunus laurocerasus	Common Laurel	White	Do.
25 Cupressus sempervirum	Common Cypress	Mixed	Do.
26 ———— disticha	Deciduous Cypress	Mixed	Do.
27 Juniperus Virginiana	Red Cedar	Mixed	Do.
28 ———— sabina	Savin Tree	Mixed	Do.
29 Salix amygdalina	Almond-leaved Willow	Mixed	Do.
30 —— vitellina	Yellow Willow	Mixed	Do.
31 Arbutus Alpina	Alpine Strawberry Tree	White	Do.
32 Rhododendron ferrugineum	Rusty-leaved Rosebay	Mixed	Do.
33 ———— hirsutum	Hairy Rosebay	Mixed	Do.

Linnean Names.	English Names.	Colour of the Blossom.	Height and Character.
34 Rhododendron ponticum	Purple Rosebay	Purple	Shrub.
35 Andromeda paniculata	Panicled Andromeda	Purple	Do.
36 Kalmia glauca	Glaucous Kalmia	Purple	Do.
37 Ledum palustre	Marsh Ledum	Mixed	Do.
38 —— decumbens	Dwarf Ledum	Mixed	Do.
39 —— latifolia	Labrador Tea	Mixed	Do.

JUNE.

1 Quercus gramuntia	Holly-leaved Oak	Mixed	Tree 50 F.
2 —— suber	Cork Tree	Mixed	Tree 30 F.
3 Fagus castanea	Spanish Chesnut	White	Tree 30 F.
4 Ficus carica	Common Fig Tree	Mixed	FruitShrub
5 Mespilus Germanica	Common Medlar	White	Tree 30 F.
6 Passiflora coerulea	Blue-flowered Passion Flower	Blue-Creeper	Shrub.
7 Clematis Virginiana	Virginian Virgin's Bower	Blue-Climber	Do.
8 Lonicera capris	Early Red Honeysuckle	Red-Climber	Do.
9 Rhus radicans	Upright Poison Oak	Cream-coloured	Do.
10 Viburnum lantana	Wayfaring Tree	White	Do.
11 Morus alba	White Mulberry Tree	Mixed	Do.
12 —— nigra	Common Mulberry	Mixed	Do.
13 —— rubra	Red Mulberry	Mixed	Do.
14 Budlea globosa	Round-headed Budlea	Yellow	Do.
15 Prunus Lusitanica	Portugal Laurel	White	Do.
16 Cornus sanguinea	Common Dogwood	Mixed	Do.
17 —— alba	White Berried Dogwood	Mixed	Do.
18 —— Sericea	Blue Berried Dogwood	Mixed	Do.
19 Rhododendron chrysanthemum	Yellow-flowered Rose Bay	Yellow	Do.
20 —— maximum	Large Rose Bay	Mixed	Do.
21 —— punctatum	Dotted Rose Bay	Mixed	Do.
22 Spartium multiflorum	Portugal White Broom	White	Do.
23 Ligustrum vulgare	Common Privet	White	Do.
24 Cistus marifolius	Marum Rock Rose	Mixed	Do.
25 —— roseus	Rose-coloured Rock Rose	Mixed	Do.
26 Andromeda hypnoides	Moss Andromeda	Mixed	Do.
27 —— mariana	Oval-leaved Andromeda	Mixed	Do.
28 Arbutus thymifolia	Thyme-leavedStrawberry-tree	White	Shrub.
29 Azalea pontica	Yellow-flowered Azalea	Yellow	Do.

H

	Linnean Names.	English Names.	Colour of the Blossoms.	Height and Character.
30	Vaccinium amœnum	Broad-leaved Wort	Pale Yellow	Very low Shrub.
31	————— venustum	Red-twigged Wort	Pale Yellow	Do.
32	————— frondosum	Obtuse-leaved Wort	Pale Blue	Do.
33	————— stamineum	Green Wood Wort	Pale Yellow	Do.
34	Erica vulgaris	Common Heath	Mixed Blue	Do.
35	Hypericum calycinum	Great-flowered St. John's Wort	Yellow	Do.

JULY.

Linnean Names.	English Names.	Colour of the Blossoms.	Height and Character.
Betula alba	Common Birch Tree	Mixed	Tree 30 F.
Punica granatum	Common Pomegranate	White with Blue Edges	Very low Shrub.
Olea Europœa	European Olive Tree	Mixed	Do.
Liriodendron tulipifera	Common Tulip Tree	Mixed	Tree 30 F.
Buxus Balearicus	Minorca Box Tree	Yellow	Very low Shrub.
Hydrangea arborescens	Tree Hydrangea	Mixed	Do.
Gaultherea procumbens	Procumbent Gaulthera	White	Do.
Andromeda pulverulenta	Powdered Andromeda	Mixed	Do.
————— polifolia	Wild Rosemary Andromeda	Purple	Do.
Kalmia latifolia	Broad leaved Kalmia	Mixed	Do.
————— angustifolia	Narrow-leaved Kalmia	Mixed	Do.

AUGUST.

Linnean Names.	English Names.	Colour of the Blossoms.	Height and Character.
Colutea arborescens	Common Bladder Senna	Yellow	Low Tree.
————— cruenta	Red-flowered Bladder Senna	Red	Do.
Stuartia Marylandica	Maryland Stuartia	White	Shrub.
Erica cinerea	Grey Heath	Mixed	Do.
Kalmia hirsuta	Hairy Kalmia	Light Blue	Do.
Erica vagaria	Cornish Heath	Mixed	Very low Shrub.

SEPTEMBER.

Linnean Names.	English Names.	Colour of the Blossoms.	Height and Character.
Robinia hispida	Rose Acacia	White	Shrub.
————— Caragana	Caragana Robinia	Mixed	Do.
Spartium junceum	Spanish Broom	Yellow	Do.
Clematis Florida	Large-flowered Virgin's Bower	White Climber	Do.
————— virticella	Purple Virgin's Bower	Purple Climber	Do.
Lavendula spicata	Common Lavender	Blue	Do.
Hyssopus officinalis	Official Hyssop	Blue	Do.

Linnean Names.	English Names.	Colour of the Blossom.	Height and Character.

OCTOBER.

Cobea scandens	Climbing Cobea..............	Purple Climber..	Shrub.
Clematis flammula	Sweet-scented Virgin's Bower	White	Do.

NOVEMBER.

Clematis vulgaris	Common Virgin's Bower	White Climber..	Shrub.

DECEMBER.

Arbutus unedo...............	Common Strawberry Tree ..	White	Shrub.
———— longifolia	Long-leaved Strawberry Tree	White	Do.
Viburnum tinus............	Lauristine Viburnum	White	Do.

Of the following list of *Herbaceous or Flowering Plants*, it is requisite to observe, that the time of flowering, though less indefinite than the height of trees, is yet apt to vary. Plants do not often come into blossom much earlier than the months herein mentioned; but they often continue to produce flowers a great deal later: thus, though there are only a few plants mentioned as flowering in November, and none in December, yet the September and October class often endure through these months. Some of the annual flowers also, especially in mild winters, and in sheltered situations, will continue in perfection till destroyed by frost. Such prolongation of their inflorescence, however, is seldom desirable, because unattended with the principal characteristics of flowers, delicacy of shape or colour, and fragrance. The season also is less adapted for perceiving their beauties.

HERBACEOUS PLANTS.

Linnean Names.	English Names.	Colour of the Blossom.	Duration.

JANUARY.

1 Helleborus niger	Christmas Rose	White	Perennial

FEBRUARY.

1 Helleborus hyemalis	Winter Aconite	White	Perennial

MARCH.

1 Helleborus viridis	Green Hellebore	Mixed	Perennial
2 Scilla Siberica	Siberian Squill	Blue	Perennial
3 Narcissus pseudo narcissus	Daffodil	Yellow	Perennial
4 ——— albus	White Narcissus	White	Perennial
5 ——— calinthus	Yellow-flowered Narcissus	Yellow	Perennial
6 ——— tarzetta	Polyanthus Narcissus	Yellow	Perennial
7 ——— jonquilla	Jonquil	Yellow	Perennial
	And many varieties		
8 Saxifraga crassifolia	Thick-leaved Saxifrage	Blue	Perennial
9 ———cordifolia	Heart-leaved Saxifrage	Blue	Perennial
10 Anemone hepatica	Common Hepatica	Blue	Perennial

APRIL.

1 Caltha palustris	Common Marsh Marygold	Yellow	Perennial
2 Tulipa sylvestris	Single Yellow Tulip	Yellow	Perennial
3 ——— Gesneriana	Common Tulip	Mixed	Perennial
4 Hyacinthus cernuus	Nodding Hyacinth	Blue	Perennial
5 ——— orientalis	Common Hyacinth	Light Blue	Perennial
6 ——— muscaria	Musk Hyacinth	Mixed	Perennial
7 ——— comosus	Purple Grape	Purple	Perennial
8 ——— botryoides	Blue Grape	Blue	Perennial
9 Anemone hortensis	Garden Anemone	Mixed	Perennial
10 ——— ranuncloides	Yellow-flowered Anemone	Yellow	Perennial
11 Saxifraga umbrosa	London Pride	Mixed	Perennial
12 Primula veris	Cowslip	Mixed	Perennial
13 ——— vulgaris	Common Primrose	Pale Yellow	Perennial
14 ——— elatior	Oxlip Primrose	Mixed	Perennial
15 ——— longifolia	Long-leaved Primrose	Mixed	Perennial
16 ——— villosa	Villous Primrose	Mixed	Perennial
17 ——— nivalis	Snowy Primrose	Mixed	Perennial
18 ——— marginata	Margined Primrose	Mixed	Perennial

Linnean Names.	English Names.	Colour of the Blossom.	Duration.
19 Primula auricula	Common Auricula in great variety	Mixed	Perennial
20 Gentiana verna	Spring Gentian	Blue	Perennial
21 ——— acaulis	Gentianella	Purple	Perennial

MAY.

1 Verbascum ferrugineum	Rusty Mullin	Mixed	Perennial
2 Aconitum napellus	Common Monk's Hood	Blue	Perennial
3 Thalictrum alpinum	Alpine Meadow Rue	Cream-coloured	Perennial
4 Aquilegia vulgaris	Common Columbine	Mixed	Perennial
5 ——— viridiflora	Green-flowered Columbine	Green	Perennial
6 Hemerocallis cærulea	Blue-flowered Day Lily	Blue	Perennial
7 Boraga orientalis	Perennial Borage	Purple	Perennial
8 Ranunculus aconitifolius	Aconite Crowfoot	White	Perennial
9 ——— platanifolius	Plane Tree-leaved Crowfoot	Yellow	Perennial
10 ——— Asiaticus	Garden Crowfoot	Mixed	Perennial
11 Lamium album	White Archangel	White	Perennial
12 ——— purpurea	Purple Archangel	Purple	Perennial
13 Cheiranthus cheri	Wall Flower	Yellow	Perennial
14 Hesperis inodora	Scentless Rocket	White	Perennial
15 Ferraria pavonia	Spotted Pavonia	Scarlet	Perennial
16 Cortusa mathioli	Broad-leaved Bear's Ear Sanicle	Pale Scarlet	Perennial
17 Potentilla aurea	Golden Cinquefoil	Yellow	Perennial
18 Helonias bulata	Spear-leaved Helonias	Mixed	Perennial
19 Phlox glaberrima	Red Flowering Lychnidea	Red	Perennial
20 ——— divaricata	Early Blue Lychnidea	Blue	Perennial
21 Hyacinthus monstrosus	Feathered Hyacinth	Blue	Perennial
22 Saxifraga Pennsylvanica	Pennsylvanian Saxifrage	Mixed	Perennial
23 ——— hirsuta	Hairy Saxifrage	Mixed	Perennial
24 Fumaria formosa	Red-flowered Fumitory	Red	Perennial
25 ——— nobilis	Large-flowered Fumitory	Mixed	Perennial
26 Primula cortusoides	Cortusa-leaved Primrose	Mixed	Perennial
27 ——— Helvetica	Swiss Primrose	Mixed	Perennial
28 ——— integrifolia	Entire-leaved Primrose	Mixed	Perennial

JUNE.

1 Helianthus annuus	Annual Sunflower	Yellow	Annual
2 Delphinium elatum	Bee Larkspur	Purple	Perennial

	Linnean Names.	English Names.	Colour of the Blossom.	Duration.
3	Delphinium exaltatum	American Larkspur	Blue	Perennial
4	Aconitum cammarum	Purple Wolfsbane	Purple	Perennial
5	Digitalis lutea	Yellow Snapdragon	Yellow	Perennial
6	Lychnis chalcedonica	Scarlet Lychnis	Scarlet	Perennial
7	—— flos-cuculi	Ragged Robin	Mixed	Perennial
8	Hemerocallis flava	Bright Yellow Day Lily	Yellow	Perennial
9	Ornithogalum lacteum	White-flowered Star of Beth-lehem	White	Perennial
10	Borago officinalis	Common Borage	Blue	Annual
11	—— Indica	Indian Borage	Mixed	Annual
12	Centaurea montana	Mountain Centaury	Blue	Perennial
13	—— cyanus	Blue Bottle	Blue	Annual
14	—— crupina	Black-seeded Centaurea	Mixed	Annual
15	Delphinium ajacis	Rocket Larkspur	Mixed White	Annual
16	—— consolida	Branching Larkspur	Blue	Annual
17	Dracæna borealis	Oval-leaved Dracæna	Green	Perennial
18	Scabiosa alpina	Alpine Scabious	Mixed	Perennial
19	—— integrifolia	Red-flowered Scabious	Red	Annual
20	—— Tartarica	Tartarian Scabious	Mixed	Perennial
21	—— Columbaria	Fine-leaved Scabious	Mixed	Perennial
22	—— Palestina	Palestine Scabious	Mixed	Annual
23	Lilium chalcedonicum	Scarlet Martagon Lily	Scarlet	Perennial
24	—— martagon	Purple Martagon Lily	Purple	Perennial
25	—— bulbiferum	Bulb-bearing Lily	Mixed	Perennial
26	—— superbum	Superb Lily	White	Perennial
27	—— aurantium	Orange Lily	Yellow	Perennial
28	—— candicans	White Lily	White	Perennial
29	Papaver dubium	Smooth Poppy	Mixed	Annual
30	Convolvulus arvensis	Corn Bind Weed	Mixed Creeper	Perennial
31	—— panduratus	Virginian Bind Weed	Mixed	Perennial
32	Pæonia albiflora	White-flowered Paeony	White	Perennial
33	Ophrys liliifolia	Lilly-leaved Ophrys	Mixed	Perennial
34	Convallaria latifolia	Broad-leaved Solomon's Seal	White	Perennial
35	—— majalis	Lily of the Valley	White	Perennial
36	Convolvulus tricolor	Three-coloured Convolvulus	Mixed	Annual
37	—— siculus	Small-flowered Convolvulus	Mixed	Annual
38	Dianthus barbatus	Sweet William Pink	Mixed	Perennial
39	—— fragrans	Fragrant Pink	Mixed	Perennial
40	Anemone palmata	Palmated Anemone	White	Perennial

Linnean Names.	English Names.	Colour of the Blossoms.	Duration.
41 Auricula farinosa	Bird Eye Primrose	Mixed	Perennial
42 Viola pedata	Multifid Violet	Purple	Perennial
43 Gentiana purpurea	Purple Gentian	Purple	Perennial

JULY.

1 Convolvulus tridentatus	Three-toothed	Mixed	Perennial
2 Campanula rotundifolia	Round-leaved Bell Flower	Blue	Perennial
3 Hemerocallis fulva	Copper-coloured Day Lily	Copper-coloured	Perennial
4 ——— graminea	Grass-leaved Day Lily	Mixed	Perennial
5 Digitalis purpurea	Purple Fox Glove	Purple	Perennial
6 Malva alcea	Vervain Mallow	Mixed	Perennial
7 —— moschata	Musk Mallow	Mixed	Perennial
8 Catananche cœrulea	Greek Valerian	Blue	Perennial
9 ——— lutea	Yellow-flowered Catananche	Yellow	Annual
10 Nicotianum tabacum	Virginian Tobacco	Cream-coloured	Annual
11 ——— rustica	Common Tobacco	Cream-coloured	Annual
12 Silene Anglica	English Catchfly	Mixed Blue	Annual
13 —— clorantha	Pale-flowered Catchfly	Pale Blue	Perennial
14 Arundo donax	Manured Reed Grass	Cream-coloured	Perennial
15 ——— colorata	Striped Reed Grass	Cream-coloured	Perennial
16 Centaurea moschata	Sweet Sultan	Mixed	Annual
17 ——— suaveolens	Yellow Sultan	Yellow	Annual
18 Chrysanthemum argentum	Silvery Chrysanthemum	White	Perennial
19 Tagetus patula	French Marygold	Yellow	Annual
20 ——— erecta	African Marygold	Yellow	Annual
21 Zinnia verticillata	Whorl-leaved Zinnia	Scarlet	Annual
22 Orchis ciliaris	Fringed Orchis	Yellow	Perennial
23 Dianthus armeria	Deptford Pink	Mixed	Annual
24 ——— prolifera	Proliferous Pink	Mixed	Annual
25 ——— diminutus	Small-flowered Pink	Mixed	Annual
26 ——— hortensis	Garden Pink in great variety	Mixed	Perennial
27 ——— Chinensis	Indian Pink	Mixed	Perennial
28 Gentiana Catesbœi	Catesby's Gentian	Blue	Perennial

AUGUST.

1 Onopordum Acantheum	Common Cotton Thistle	Mixed	Perennial
2 Helianthus tubæformis	Tube-flowered Sunflower	Yellow	Annual

Linnean Names.	English Names.	Colour of the Blossoms.	Duration.
3 Aster umbellata	Umbel-flowered Starwort	Mixed	Perennial
4 —— amellus	Italian Starwort	Mixed	Perennial
5 Campanula grandiflora	Great-flowered Bell Flower	Light Blue	Perennial
6 —— latifolia	Broad-leaved Bell Flower	Blue	Perennial
7 Mentha piperita	Peppermint	Mixed	Perennial
8 Phlox paniculata	Panicled Lychnidea	Light Blue	Perennial
9 —— suaveolens	White-flowered Lychnidea	White	Perennial
10 Chelone obliquæ	Red-flowered Chelone	Red	Perennial
11 Zinnia violacea	Purple-flowered Zinnia	Purple	Perennial
12 Amaranthus hypochondriacus	Prince's Feather	Red	Annual
13 —————— caudatus	Love lies Bleeding	Red	Annual

SEPTEMBER.

1 Aster foliosus	Leafy Starwort	Mixed	Perennial
2 —— longifolius	Long-leaved Starwort	Mixed	Perennial
3 Campanula versicolor	Various-coloured Bell Flower	Mixed	Perennial
4 —— pulla	Dark-flowered Bell Flower	Blue	Perennial
5 Lychnis Diurna	Red-flowered Lychnis	Red	Perennial
6 Antirrhinum purpureum	Purple Snapdragon	Purple	Perennial
7 Dahlia pinnata	Elder-leaved Dahlia	Scarlet	Perennial
8 —— coccinea	Red-flowered Dahlia	Red	Perennial
9 Crocus officinalis	Saffron Crocus	Mixed	Perennial
10 —— nudiflorus	Naked-flowered Crocus	Mixed	Perennial

OCTOBER.

1 Aster grandiflorus	Great-flowered Starwort	Mixed	Perennial
2 —— seratorius	Late-flowering Starwort	Mixed	Perennial
3 —— junceus	Rush-stalked Starwort	Mixed	Perennial
4 —— pendulus]	Pendulus Starwort	Mixed	Perennial
5 —— flexuosus	Zigzag Starwort	Mixed	Perennial
6 Fumaria lutea	Yellow-flowered Fumitory	Yellow	Perennial

NOVEMBER.

1 Cherianthus annus	Ten-week Stock	White	Annual
2 —————— incanus	Branton Stock	White	Annual
3 Crocus cerotinus	Late-flowering Crocus	Mixed	Perennial
4 Antirrhinum Cymbalaria	Ivy-leaved Snapdragon	Blue	Perennial

3. SELECT LIST OF FRUIT TREES AND FRUIT SHRUBS.

In selecting a list of fruits, suitable for the gardens of small villas, regard has been had more to the quantity and excellence of the fruit, than to the variety of sorts. Such trees as are *approved bearers*, whose fruit is of *acknowledged superiority*, and which will produce a *crop in most seasons*, are therefore alone introduced. Those who wish for a more extensive assortment, will find their taste amply gratified, by applying for any nurseryman's catalogue; though it has been justly questioned whether out of every hundred different names of apples and gooseberries, there will be found more than fifty distinguishable varieties.

Those marked thus * are preferable.

ALMONDS.

NAMES.	ASPECT, &c.	NAMES.	ASPECT, &c.
Bitter fruited		Silver-leaved	
Sweet do.		Silver-striped-leaved	

APPLES.

NAMES.	ASPECT, &c.	NAMES.	ASPECT, &c.
* Golden Pippin	S. E. or W.	* Oslin Pippin	E. or W. and Esp. or St.
* Downton Pippin	S. E. or W.	* Ribstone do.	S. E. or W. and Esp. or St.
(an improved variety of the Golden)		Gogar do.	Esp. and St. or S. E. or W.
* Ribston Pippin	Esp. or St.		
Kentish do.	Esp. or St.	* Nonpareil	S. S. E. or S. W.
* Golden Russet	S. E. or W.	Yorkshire Greening	E. W. or N.
* Royal Russet	E. or. W. and Esp. or St.	Codling	Esp. or St.
		Dutch Codling	Esp. or St.
Wheeler's Russet	Esp. or St.	* Carlisle do.	Esp. or St.
Newton Pippin	S. E. W.		

I

NAMES.	ASPECT, &c.	NAMES.	ASPECT, &c.
Kentish do. .... Esp. or St.		* Grey do. .... Esp. or St.	
* Royal do. .... Esp. or St.		* Summer Queening... Esp. or St.	
* Royal Pearmain .... Esp. or St.		* Winter do. .... Esp. or St.	
* Summer Pearmain... Esp. or St.		* Yorkshire Green.... Esp. or St.	
* Loan's do. .... Esp. or St.		Lady Wemyss .... Esp. or St.	
* Golden Rennet ....S. or Esp. or St.		* Norfolk Beafing .... Esp. or St.	
Nonsuch .... Esp. or St.		Strawberry .... Esp. or St.	
Green Leadington ....Esp. or St.		Pursemouth .... Esp. or St.	
Yellow do. .... Esp. or St.			

APRICOTS.

* Mere Park ....S. E. or W.		* Orange ... . S. E. or W.	
Roman .... S. E. or W.		Turkey.............. S. E. or W.	
* Brussels .... S. E. or W.		* Breda .... S. E. or W.	

CHERRIES.

* May Duke ....N. E. S. W. or Esp. or St.		* Holman's Duke .....S. E. W. and Esp. or St.	
Arch Duke .... S. E. W.		* Morella .... N. E. W. and Esp. or St.	
* Black Heart ....S. E. W. and Esp. or St.		Harrison's Heart......S. E. W.	
* White Heart........S. E. W. and Esp. or St.		* Kentish .... N. E. W. and Esp. or St.	

CURRANTS.

Red Dutch	Champaign
White Dutch	Black

FIGS.

* Blue Ischia ....S. E. or W.		White do.............S.	
* Brown do. ....S.		Black Genoa ....S.	

GOOSEBERRIES.

Early Green Gooseberry	Raspberry
Early White Dutch	Amber
Smooth Red	Rumbullion
Hertfordshire Red	Green Gage
Claret	Red Champaign
Damson	Hunt's Primo
Large White	Large Crystal

NAMES.	ASPECT, &c.	NAMES.	ASPECT, &c.
Late Dutch		Bellmont Red	
Green Griffin			

Besides the above there are numerous Lancashire Gooseberries of a very large size.

GRAPES.

White Sweet Water	Syrian
White Muscadine	White Raisin
Royal do.	Red do.
Black do.	Black Constantia
White Tokay	White do.
Flame-coloured Tokay	White Muscat of Alexandria
White Frontinac	Black Muscat
Black do.	Large Black Cluster
Red do.	White Passe Mosque
Grisly do.	Grecian or Greek Grape
White Hamburgh or Portugal	St. Peter's Grape
Black Hamburgh	Lombardy

NECTARINES.

* Elruge	.............S. E. or W.	Murray	...............S. E. or W.
* Duc de Tello	........S. E. or W.	Scarlet	...............S. E. or W.

PEACHES.

* Red Magdalen	.......S. E. or W.	* Montabon	..........S. E. or W.
* Noblesse	...........S. E. or W.	* Admirable	..........S. E. or W.

PEARS.

* Jargonelle	..........S. E. or W. or Esp. or St.	* Achan	...............E. or W. Esp. or St.
Summer Bergamot	..... S. E. W. or Esp. or St.	St. Germains	.........E. or W.
		Chaumontelle	.........S.
* Autumn Bergamot	...S. E. or W.	* Moorfowl Egg	......Esp. or St.
Scotch Bergamot	.......Esp. or St.	* Yair	................E. W. Esp. or St.
* Gansell's Bergamet	..S. E. W. Esp. or St.	* Green Yair	..........N. E. W.
* Swiss do.	...........S. E. W.	Terling	................S. E. W.
* Cressane do.	.........S. E. W.	Colmar	..............S. E. W.
* Burie de Roy	......S. E. W.	* Carnock	............Esp. or St.
Swan Egg	.............E. W. Esp. or St.	Warden	..............N. E. W. or Esp. or St.
* Grey Achan	.........N. E. W. Esp. or St.	Longueville	............Esp. or St.

NAMES.	ASPECT, &c.	NAMES.	ASPECT, &c.
* Black Worcester	N. E. W. or Esp. or St.	* Craaford	Esp. or St.
		Drummond	Esp. or St.
Cadilac	N. E. W. or Esp. or St.	Lammas	Esp. or St.

PLUMS.

* Green Gage	S. E. W. Esp. or St.	* Orlean	Esp. or St.
* Yellow do.	S. E. W.	Drap d' or	Esp. or St.
* Blue do.	E. W.	* Fotheringham	E. W. Esp. or St.
* White Magnum Bo-		* Wine, sour	Esp. or St.
num —	S. E. W. Esp. or St.	Blue Perdrigon	Esp. or St.
Red do. do.	E. W. Esp. or St.	* Damask	Esp. or St.
* La Royale	S.	* Bullace	Esp. or St.
* Imperatrice	S. E. W.		

RASPBERRIES.

Red fruited   White fruited
Large Red or Cone   Antwerp
Twice-bearing Red

STRAWBERRIES.

Red Wood   Hautboy Strawberry
White do.   Green or Pine
Red Alpine   Chili
White do.   White Bath
Virginian or Scarlet

4. CATALOGUE OF TREES, SHRUBS, AND HERBACEOUS PLANTS,

Adapted for Plantations and Pleasure Grounds, with the London Prices of 1812.

The information here offered is the result of considerable assiduity and experience in this branch of horticultural science; the prices however must be considered as approximating rather than obtaining complete exactness, which is barely possible in a subject so varying in its nature, and depending obviously upon adventitious circumstances. The list has been formed upon an average view of the most respectable nurserymen's charges, and it is confidently believed will be found sufficiently correct for all practical purposes.

PRICED CATALOGUE OF TREES, SHRUBS, &c.

H. T. denotes handsome trees; that is, such sorts as are peculiarly adapted for ornamental purposes.

Com. Sh. common shrubs, for ordinary purposes.

Ev. sh. evergreen shrubs.

Amer. American shrubs, or trees growing little larger than shrubs, requiring peat soil to bring them into free growth.

Acer hybridum, 1s. 6d. H. T.
—— opalus, 1s. 6d. H. T.
—— criticum, 1s. 6d. H. T.
—— laciniatum, 1s. H. T.
—— montanum, 1s. 6d. H. T.
—— negundo, 1s. H. T.
—— pallidum, 1s. H. T.
—— palmatum, 2s. 6d. H. T.
—— Pennsylvanicum, 2s. 6d. H. T.
—— rubrum, 1s. H. T.
—— sacharinum, 1s. H. T.
—— Tartaricum, 1s. 6d. H. T.
—— variegatum, 1s. 6d. H. T.
Æsculus flava, 1s. 6d. H. T.
—— parvi-flora, 10s. 6d. Amer.
—— pavia, 2s. 6d. H. T.
Ailanthus glandulosa, 1s. 6d. H. T.
Amorpha fruticosa, 1s. 6d. com. sh.
Amygdalus amara, 2s. 6d. H. T.
—— communis, 2s. 6d. H. T.
—— nana, 1s. 6d. com. sh.
—— orientalis, 2s. 6d. com. sh.
—— Persica, 3s. com. sh.
—— pumila, 1s. 6d. com. sh.

Andromeda acuminata, 2s. 6d. ev. sh. Amer.
—— angustifolia, 3s. 6d. Amer.
—— auxiliaris, 2s. 6d. ev. sh. Amer.
—— calyculata, 1s. 6d. ev. sh. Amer.
—— cassinefolia, 21s. Amer.
—— coriacea, 7s. 6d. ev. sh. Amer.
—— Catesbæi, 7s. 6d. Amer.
—— dabœcia, 1s. 6d. Amer.
—— dealbati, 21s. Amer.
—— erecta, 1s. 6d. ev. sh. Amer.
—— latifolia, 1s. 6d. ev. sh.
—— lucida, 7s. 6d. ev. sh. Amer.
—— mariana, 5s. Amer.
—— paniculata, 2s. 6d. Amer.
—— platanifolia, 1s. 6d. Amer.
—— polifolia, 1s. 6d. ev. sh. Amer.
—— racemosa, 2s. 6d. Amer.
Annona triloba, 5s. Amer.
Aralia spinosa, 5s. Amer.
Arbutus andrachne, 7s. 6d. ev. sh.
—— andrachne serratus, 7s. 6d. ev. sh.
—— crispa, 7s. 6d. ev. sh.
—— rubra, 5s. ev. sh.
—— thymifolia, 5s. ev. sh. Amer.

6

Arbutus unedo, 1s. 6d. H. T. ev. sh.
—— uva ursi 2s. 6d. ev. sh. Amer.
Atriplex halimus, 6d. com. sh.
Azalea bicolor, 5s. Amer.
—— carnia, 5s. Amer.
—— erecta, 5s. Amer.
—— fissa, 5s. Amer.
—— floribunda, 5s. Amer.
—— glauca, 2s. 6d. Amer.
—— glauca scabra, 5s. Amer.
—— nudiflora fastigiata, 7s. 6d. Amer.
—— nudiflora papilonacea, 5s. Amer.
—— papilonacea nudiflora var. 5s. Amer.
—— nudiflora staminibus rubris, 5s. Amer.
—— nudiflora orange, 7s. 6d. Amer.
—— nudiflora pleno, 5s. Amer.
—— pontica, 7s. 6d. Amer.
—— præcox, 5s. Amer.
—— procumbens, 7s. 6d. Amer.
—— rubra, 5s. Am. sh.
—— rubra odorata, 5s. Am. sh.
—— rubra, scarlet, 7s. 6d. Am. sh.
—— salicifolia, 5s. Am. sh.
—— tomentosa, 2s. 6d. Am. sh.
—— viscosa variegata, 10s. 6d. Am. sh.
Berberis Canadensis, 3s. 6d. com. sh.
—— critica, 1s. 6d. com. sh.
—— vulgaris, 6d. com. sh.
Betula angulata, 1s. 6d. H. T.
—— glauca, 1s. 6d. H. T.
—— ignerica, 1s. 6d. H. T.
—— lacinata, 1s. 6d. H. T.
—— nana, 1s. com. sh.
—— oblongata, 1s. 6d. H. T.
—— papyracia, 1s. 6d. H. T.
—— pendula, 1s. H. T.
—— populifolia, 1s. 6d. H. T.
—— pumila, H. T.
Bignonia catalpa, 1s. 6d. H. T.
Bupleurum fruticosum, 1s. com. sh.

Baxus angustifolia, 1s. ev. sh.
—— Balearicus 1s. 6d. com. ev. sh.
—— marginata, 6s. ev. sh.
—— myrtifolia, 1s. com. sh.
—— sempervirens, 6s. com. ev. sh.
—— variegata, 1s. com. ev. sh.
Calycanthus florida, 1s. 6d. Am. sh.
Carpinus ostyra, 1s. 6d. H. T.
—— Virginiana, 1s. 6d. H. T.
Ceanothus Americanus, 1s. 6d. Am. sh.
Celtis occidentalis, 1s. 6d. H. T.
Cephalanthus occidentalis, 1s. 6d. Am. sh.
Cercis siliquastrum, 2s. 6d. H. T.
Chionanthus Virginicus, 3s. 6d. Am. sh.
Cistus helianthemum, var. each 1s. 6d. Am. sh.
—— incanus, 1s. 6d. com. sh.
—— ladaniferus, 1s. 6d. ev. sh.
—— laurifolius, 1s. 6d. ev. sh.
—— ledon, 1s. com. sh.
—— mutabilis, 1s. 6d. Am. sh.
—— populifolius, 1s. 6d. com. ev. sh.
—— salicifolius, 1s. 6d. com. sh.
—— 20 other sorts, 1s. 6d. each, com. sh.
Clethra alnifolia, 1s. 6d. Am. sh.
—— paniculata, 2s. 6d. Am. sh.
—— pubescens, 2s. 6d. Am. sh.
Colutea arborescens, 4d. com. sh.
—— Pocockii, 1s. 6d. com. sh.
Comptonia asplenifolia, 1s. 6d. Am. sh.
Coriaria myrtifolia, 6s. com. sh.
Cornus alba, 4d. com. sh.
—— alternifolia, 1s. com. sh.
—— mascula, 6s. sh.
—— paniculata, 1s. com. sh.
—— florida, 1s. 6d. Am. sh.
—— rossica, 6d. com. sh.
—— sanguinea, 4d. com. sh.
—— sericea, 6d. com. sh.
—— stricta, 6s. com. sh.
—— variegata, 6s. com. sh.
Corylus columna, 2s. 6d. H. T.

Corylus rostrata, 1s. 6d. com. sh.
Coronilla emerus, 6s. com. sh.
Cratægus aria, 1s. 6d. H. T.
———— aria dentata, 1s. 6d. H. T.
———— aurifolia, 2s. 6d. H. T.
———— azarolus, 2s. 6d. H. T.
———— coccinea, 3s. 6d. H. T.
———— cordata, 2s. 6d. H. T.
———— crusgalli splendus, 2s. 6d. H. T.
———— crusgalli pyracanthafolia, 3s. 6d. H. T.
———— elliptica, 2s. 6d. H. T.
———— flava, 2s. 6d. H. T.
———— glandulosa, 3s. 6d. H. T.
———— hybrida, 2s. 6d. H. T.
———— incisa, 3s. 6d. H. T.
———— odoratissima, 3s. 6d. H. T.
———— oxyacantha aurea, 2s. 6d. H. T.
———— parvifolia, 2s. 6d. H. T.
———— pleno, 2s. 6d. H. T.
———— præcox, 2s. 6d. H. T.
———— punctata, 1s. 6d. H. T.
———— pyrifolia, 2s. 6d. H. T.
———— rubra, 2s. 6d. H. T.
———— sanguinea, 3s. 6d. H. T.
———— salicifolia, 3s. 6d. H. T.
———— Suecia, 2s. 6d. H. T.
———— tanacetifolia, 2s. 6d. H. T.
———— torminalis, 2s. 6d. H. T.
Cupressus disticha, 2s. 6d. H. T.
———— horizontalis, 1s. 6d. ev. sh.
———— pendula, 5s. H. T.
———— sempervirens, 1s. 6d. H. T.
———— thyoides, 1s. 6d. H. T.
Cytisus capitatus argenteus, 1s. 6d. com. sh.
———— capitatus biflorus, 1s. 6d. com. sh.
———— laburnum, 6s. H. T.
———— nigricans, 1s. com. sh.

Cytisus purpureus, 1s. 6d. com. sh.
———— sempervirens, 6s. com. sh.
———— sessilifolius, 6s. com. sh.
———— var. latifidum, 1s. H. T.
Daphne Alpina, 2s. 6d. Amer. sh.
———— autumnalis, 2s. 6d. Amer. sh.
———— cneorum, var. 3s. 6d. ev. sh. Amer.
———— collina, 2s. 6d. ev. sh. Amer.
———— creonem, 2s. 6d. Amer. sh.
———— gnidium, 5s. Amer. sh.
———— laureola, 6s. com. ev. sh.
———— mezerion, red, 1s. com. sh.
———— mezerion, white, 1s. com. sh.
———— pontica, 5s. ev. sh. Amer.
———— tartonraira, 5s. Amer. sh.
Dirca palustris, 5s. Amer. sh.
Diospyros Virginiana, 1s. 6d. H. T.
Eleagnus angustifolius, 1s. 6d. H. T.
Empetrum nigrum, 1s. 6d. ev. sh. Amer.
———— Scoticum, 1s. 6d. Amer. sh.
Ephedra disticha, 1s. 6d. ev. sh. Amer.
———— monostachya, 1s. 6d. ev. sh. Amer.
Erica alba, 1s. 6d.
———— australis, 2s. 6d. ev. sh. Amer.
———— ciliaris, 1s. 6d. ev. sh. Amer.
———— cinerea alba, 1s. 6d. ev. sh.
———— dabœcia, 1s. 8d. ev. sh.
———— herbacea, 1s. 6d. ev. sh. Amer.
———— Mediterranea, 1s. 6d. ev. sh. Amer.
———— multiflora, 5s. ev. sh.
———— stricta, 1s. 6d. ev. sh. Amer.
———— tetralix alba, 1s. 6d. ev. sh. Amer.
———— vagans, 1s. 6d. ev. sh. Amer.
———— vagans alba, 1s. 6d. ev. sh. Amer.
———— vulgaris alba, 1s. 6d. ev. sh. Amer.
———— vulgaris pleno, 1s. 6d. ev. sh. Amer.
———— umbellato, 2s. 6d. ev. sh. Amer.
Euonymus Americanus, 1s. 6d. com. ev. sh.

(64)

Euonymus angustifolius, 1s. 6d. Amer. sh.
——— atropurpureus, 1s. 6d. Amer. sh.
——— Europæus, 6d. com. sh.
——— fructa alba, 1s. com. sh.
——— latifolius, 1s. 6d. com. sh.
——— sempervirens, 1s. 6d. Am. sh.
——— verrucosus, 1s. 6d. com. sh.
Fagus asplenifolia, 7s. 6d. H. T.
—— ferruginea, 5s. H. T.
—— pumila, 5s. Am. sh.
—— purpurea, 2s. 6d. H. T.
Fothergilla alnifolia, 3s. 6d. Amer. sh.
——— glauca, 5s. Amer. sh.
Fraxinus Americanus, 1s. 8d. H. T.
——— atra, 2s. 6d. H. T.
——— Chinensis, 1s. 6d. H. T.
——— diversifolius, 1s. 6d. H. T.
——— ornus, 1s. 6d. H. T.
——— pendulus, 2s. 6d. H. T.
Gaultheria procumbens, 1s. 6d. ev. sh.
Amer.
——— florida, 6d. com. sh.
Genista Germanica, 1s. 6d. com. ev. sh.
——— linifolia, 6s. com. sh.
——— sagittalis, 1s. 6d. ev. sh.
——— triquetra, 1s. 6d. com. ev. sh.
Gleditsia horrida, 5s. H. T.
——— triacanthos, 1s. H. T.
Glycine frutescens, 3s. 6d. Amer. sh.
Gordonia pubescens, 5s. Amer. sh.
Guilandina, bonduc, 7s. 6d. H. T.
Halesia tetraptera, 5s. Amer. sh.
Hamamelis Virginica, 1s. 6d. Amer. sh.
Hedera helix, 3d. ev. sh.
——— Hibernia rubra, 1s. 6d. ev. sh.
——— Hibernia virida, 1s. 6d. ev. sh.
——— pontica, 1s. 6d. ev. sh.
Hibiscus albo pleno, 2s. 6d. com. sh.
——— Syriacus, purple, 6s. com. sh.
——— Syriacus, red, 6s. com. sh.

Hibiscus Syriacus, white, 6s. com. sh.
——— Syriacus, painted lady, 6s. com.
sh.
——— Syriacus, fol. var. 1s. 6d. com. sh.
——— Syriacus rubra pleno, 1s. 6d. com. sh.
Hippophæ rhamnoides, 6s. com. sh.
Hydrangea cœrulea, 5s. Amer. sh.
——— glauca, 2s. 6d. Amer. sh.
——— quercifolia, 2s. 6d. Amer. sh.
Hypericum calycinum, 4d. com. ev. sh.
——— prolificum, 1s. 1d. Amer. sh.
Jasminum fruticans, 4d. com. sh.
——— humile, 1s. com. sh.
——— officinale, 6s. com. sh.
Ilex aquifolium, 6s. com. ev. sh.
—— folium, var. 1s. 6d. ev. sh.
—— opaca, 5s. ev. sh. Amer.
—— prinoides, 1s. 6d. Amer. sh.
Striped hollies in great var. 1s. 6d. com.
sh.
Do. large plants, 8s. com. sh.
Itea virginea, 1s. 6d. Amer. sh.
Juglans regia, ten sorts, each 1s. 6d. H. T.
Juniperus communis, 6d. com. ev. sh.
——— montana, 1s. 6d. com. ev. sh.
——— oxycedrus, 5s. com. ev. sh.
——— Phœnicea, 5s. ev. sh.
——— repens, 1s. 6d. com. ev. sh.
——— sabina, 6s. com. ev. sh.
——— Siberica, 1s. 6d. com. ev. sh.
——— Suecia, 1s. com. ev. sh.
——— tamariscifolius, 9d. com. ev. sh.
——— thurifera, 7s. 6d. com. ev. sh.
——— variegata, 9d. com. ev. sh.
——— Virginiana, 1s. 6d. H. T.
Kalmia angustifolia, 2s. 6d. ev. sh. Amer.
——— glauca, 2s. 6d. ev. sh. Amer.
——— latifolia, 7s. 6d. ev. sh. Amer.
——— serotina, 3s. 6d. ev. sh. Amer.
——— variegata, 3s. 6d. Amer. sh.

Laurus benzoin, 2s. 6d. Amer. sh.
——— nobilis, 1s. 6d. com. ev. sh.
——— sassafras, 7s. 6d. H. T.
Ledum buxifolium, 5s. ev. sh. Amer.
——— decumbens, 3s. 6d. ev. sh. Amer.
——— latifolium, 3s. 6d. ev. sh. Amer.
——— odoratum, 3s. 6d. ev. sh. Amer.
——— palustre, 2s. 6d. ev. sh. Amer.
Ligustrum fruct. alba, 1s. com. sh.
——— vulgare, 6d. com. sh.
——— variegata, 1s. 6d. com. sh.
Liquidamber styraciflua, 1s. 6d. H. T.
Liriodendron tulipifera, 2s. 6d. H. T.
Lonicera Alpigena, 6d. com. sh.
——— cœrulea, 4d. com. sh.
——— diervilla, 6d. com. sh.
——— early white, 6d. com. sh.
——— early red, 6d. com. sh.
——— early Dutch, 6d. com. sh.
——— evergreen, 1s. 6d. com. sh.
——— grata, 1s. 6d. ev. sh. Amer.
——— implexa, 1s. 6d. ev. sh. Amer.
——— long blowing, 6d. com. sh.
——— nigra, 4d. com. sh.
——— oak-leaved, 1s. com. sh.
——— sempervirens, 1s. 6d. Amer. sh.
——— symphora-carpos, 6d. com. sh.
——— tartarica, 1s. com. sh.
——— trumpet, 6d. com. sh.
——— xylosteum, 4d. com. sh.
Lycium barbarum, 6d. com. sh.
Magnolia acuminata, 7s. 6d. Amer. sh.
——— glauca, 7s. Amer. sh.
——— grandiflora, 5s. ev. sh. Amer.
——— angustifolia, 7s. 6d. ev. sh. Amer.
——— Exmouthia, 15s. ev. sh. Amer.
——— ferruginea, 7s. 6d. ev. sh. Amer.
——— Solandrifolia, 10s. 6d. ev. sh. Amer.

Magnolia purpurea, 7s. 6d. Amer. sh.
——— tripetala, 7s. 6d. Amer. sh.
Menispermum Canadense, 1s. 6d. Amer. sh.
——— Carolinum, 1s. 6d. Amer. sh.
Mespilus arbutifolia, 3s. 6d. H. T.
——— amelanchier, 2s. 6d. H. T.
——— Canadensis, 2s. 6d. H. T.
——— Caroliniana, 1s. 6d. com. sh.
——— chamæ mespilus, 1s. 6d. com. sh.
——— cotoneaster, com. sh.
——— grandiflora, 5s. H. T.
——— latifolia, 1s. 6d. com. sh.
——— pumila, 1s. 6d. com. sh.
——— tomentosa, 1s. 6d. com. sh.
Morus alba, 2s. 6d. H. T.
——— papyracea, 3s. 6d. com. sh.
Myrica cerifera, 1s. com. sh. Amer.
——— gale, 1s. 6d. Amer. sh.
——— latifolia, 2s. 6d. com. sh. Amer.
——— sempervirens, 1s. 6d. Amer. sh.
Nyssa integrifolia, 5s. Amer. sh.
Ononis fruticosa, 3s. 6d. Amer. sh.
Periploca Græca, 1s. com. sh.
Phyllyrea buxifolia, 1s. 6d. ev. sh.
——— latifolia, 1s. 6d. com. ev. sh.
——— ligustrifolia, 1s. 6d. ev. sh.
——— media, 1s. 6d. com. ev. sh.
——— obliqua, 1s. 6d. com. ev. sh.
——— oleafolia, 1s. 6d. ev. sh.
——— pendula, com. ev. sh.
——— romanifolia, 1s. 6d. com. ev. sh.
——— spinosa, 1s. 6d. com. ev. sh.
——— tractata, 1s. 6d. ev. sh.
Pinus abies, 6s. ev. sh.
——— tœda, 2s. 6d. H. T.
——— alba, 1s. 6d. ev. sh.
——— aleopecuroides, 3s. 6d. ev. sh.
——— balsamea, 1s. ev. sh.
——— Canadensis, 1s. 6d. H. T.
——— cedrus, 3s. 6d. H. T.

K

Pinus Coimbra, 5s. ev. sh.

—— larix, 3s. H. T.

—— mugho, 1s. 6d. ev. sh.

—— nigra, 1s. 6d. ev. sh.

—— picea, 6d. ev. sh.

—— pinaster, in pots, 1s. 6d. H. T.

—— pinea, 1s. 6d. H. T.

—— rigida, 2s. 6d. ev. sh.

—— sylvestris, 3d. ev. sh.

—— strobus, 6d. H. T.

—— variabilis, 1s. ev. sh.

—— zada, 2s. 6d. ev. sh.

Platanus Hispania, 6d. H. T.

——— occidentalis, 6d. H. T.

——— orientalis, 2s. 6d. H. T.

Polygala chamæbuxus, 3s. 6d. ev. sh. Amer.

Populus alba, 1s. H. T.

—— angulata, 1s. 6d. H. T.

—— balsamifera, 6d. H. T.

—— Græca, 1s. 6d. H. T.

—— heterophylla, 2s. 6d. H. T.

—— monolifera, 9d. H. T.

—— nigra, 6d. H. T.

—— stricta, 6d. H. T.

Prinos Caroliniana, 5s. Amer. sh.

——— glabra, 2s. 6d. ev. sh. Amer.

——— lavigata, 5s. Amer. sh.

——— verticillata, 1s. 6d. com. sh. Amer.

Prunus glabra, 3s. 6d. ev. sh.

——— laurocerasus, 4d. com. ev. sh.

——— Lusitanica, 1s. com. ev. sh.

——— mahaleb, 6d. com. sh.

——— nigra, 1s. 6d. com. sh.

——— padus, 6d. H. T.

——— pendula, 1s. 6d. H. T.

——— pumila, 1s. com. sh.

——— rubra, 2s. 6d. H. T.

——— Virginiana, 6d. com. sh.

Ptelea trifoliata, 1s. com. sh.

Pyrus angustifolia, 2s. 6d. H. T.

—— baccata, 3s. 6d. H. T.

—— coronaria, 3s. 6d. H. T.

—— pollveria, 1s. 6d. H. T.

—— præcox, 1s. 6d. H. T.

—— rubra, 2s. 6d. H. T.

—— salicifolia, 3s. 6d. H. T.

—— Siberica, 2s. 6d. H. T.

—— spectabilis, 2s. 6d. H. T.

Quercus esculentus, 5s. H. T.

——— alba, 5s. H. T.

——— alba multifida, 5s. H. T.

——— aquatica attenuata, 1s. 6d. H. T.

——— aquatica elongata, 3s. 6d. H. T.

——— aquatica cunata, 1s. 6d. H. T.

——— aquatica heterophylla, 1s. 6d. H. T.

——— aquatica incisa, 2s. 6d. H. T.

——— aquatica indivisa, 3s. 6d. H. T.

——— aquatica latifolia, 2s. 6d. H. T.

——— aquatica sinuata, 1s. 6d. H. T.

——— aquatica undulata, 3s. 6d. H. T.

——— Bannisterii, 5s. H. T.

—— candida, 5s. H. T.

——— ceres angustifolia, 9d. H. T.

——— ceres latifolia, 9d. H. T.

——— coccinea, 1s. H. T.

——— falcata, 5s. H. T.

——— ilex, 1s. 6d. ev. sh.

——— ilex latifolia, 1s. 6d.

——— ilex oblongata, 1s. 6d.

——— latifolia, 3s. 6d. H. T.

——— lyrata, 7s. 6d. H. T.

——— montana, 1s. H. T.

——— nigra, 2s. 6d. H. T.

——— oblongata, 1s. 6d. H. T.

——— obtusa, 5s. H. T.

——— obtundiloba, 10s. 6d. H. T.

——— phellos, 1s. 6d. H. T.

——— prinus, 1s. 6d. H. T.

——— robur, 3d. H. T.

Quercus rubra, 1*s.* H. T.
———— sinuata, 2*s.* 6*d.*
———— suber, 2*s.* 6*d.* H. T.
———— tenebria, 5*s.* H. T.
———— tenebria multifida, 5*s.* H. T.
———— tomentosa, 7*s.* 6*d.* H. T.
———— variegata, 5*s.* H. T.
———— virens, 5*s.* H. T.
———— zurnens, 8*s.* H. T.
Rhamnus alaternus, 1*s.* com. ev. sh.
———— alnifolius, 3*s.* 6*d.* com. sh.
———— Alpina, 1*s.* 6*d.* com. sh.
———— angustifolius, 1*s.* com. ev. sh.
———— argentia, 1*s.* 6*d.* com. ev. sh.
———— aureus, 1*s.* 6*d.* com. sh.
———— var. 1*s.* 6*d.* com. sh.
———— catharticus, 4*d.* com. sh.
———— frangula, 4*d.* com. sh.
———— insectorus, 6*d.* com. sh.
———— latifolius, 2*s.* 6*d.* com. ev. sh.
———— maculata, 1*s.* ev. sh.
———— variegatus, 1*s.* 6*d.* com. sh.
———— variegata aurea, 1*s.* 6*d.* ev. sh.
———— volubilis, 1*s.* 6*d.* com. sh.
Rhododendron dauricum, 15*s.* Amer. sh.
————————ferrugineum, 6*s.* ev. Am. sh.
————————hirsutum, 5*s.* ev. sh. Amer.
————————hirsutum variegatum, 5*s.*
          Amer. sh.
————————maximum, 8*s.* ev. sh. Am.
————————ponticum, 2*s.* 6*d.* ev. sh. Am.
————————ponticum algivensis, 2*s.* 6*d.*
          Amer. sh.
————————ponticum periculum, 5*s.*
          Amer. sh.
————————ponticum variegatum, 6*s.*
          Amer. sh.
————————pudatum, 5*s.* Amer. sh.
————————punctatum, 5*s.* ev. sh.
————————variegatum, 5*s.* ev. sh.
4

Rhodora Canadensis, 1*s.* 6*d.* Amer. sh.
Rhus copalinum, 2*s.* 6*d.* com. sh.
———— cotinus, 6*d.* com. sh.
———— eleagnus, 1*s.* 6*d.* H. T.
———— glabrum, 1*s.* 6*d.* com. sh.
——— typhinum, 1*s.* H. T.
———— vernix, 1*s.* 6*d.* H. T.
Ribes Alpinum, 4*d.* com. sh.
———— cynosbati, 6*d.* com. sh.
Robinia atragana, 2*s.* 6*d.* com. sh. Amer.
———— caragana, 1*s.* 6*d.* com. sh.
——— chamlagu, 2*s.* 6*d.* Amer. sh.
———— glutinosa, 1*s.* 6*d.* H. T.
———— halodendron, 5*s.* com. sh. Amer.
———— hispida, 1*s.* 6*d.* com. sh.
———— pseud-acacia, 6*d.* H. T.
———— pubescens, 1*s.* 6*d.* Amer. sh.
———— spinosa, 2*s.* 6*d.* com. sh. Amer.
Rosa blanda, 1*s.* 6*d.* Amer. sh.
——— ferox, 3*s.* 6*d.* Amer. sh.
——— Levant, 5*s.* Amer. sh.
——— Rhanexhaticus, 1*s.* 6*d.* Amer. sh.
——— sempervirens, 1*s.* ev. sh.
Rosmarinus officinatis, 1*s.* ev. sh.
Rubus apifolius, 1*s.* com. sh.
——— arcticus, 1*s.* 6*d.* Amer. sh.
——— fruticosus, 1*s.* 6*d.* com. sh.
——— odoratus, 4*d.* com. sh.
Ruscus aculeatus, 1*s.* com. ev. sh.
——— racemosus, 2*s.* 6*d.* com. ev. sh.
Smilax aspera, 2*s.* 6*d.* ev. sh. Amer.
——— lanceolata, 5*s.* ev. sh. Amer.
——— rotundifolia, 5*s.* Amer. sh.
——— tamoides, 3*s.* 6*d.* Amer. sh.
Sorbus acuparia, 6*d.* H. T.
——— domestica, 3*s.* 6*d.* H. T.
Spartium argenteum, 5*s.* com. sh.
————— decumbens, 1*s.* 6*d.* com. sh.
————— flora pleno, 1*s.* 6*d.* com. sh.
————— junceum, 4*d.* com. ev. sh.

Spartium multiflorum, 6d. com. ev. sh.
———— radiatum, 3s. 6d. com. sh.
Spiræa chamœdrifolia, 2s. 6d. Amer. sh.
———— crenata, 1s. 6d. Amer. sh.
———— daurica, 3s. Amer. sh.
———— hypericifolia, 6d. com. sh.
———— lævigata, 1s. 6d. Amer. sh.
———— opulifolia, 6d. com. sh.
———— paniculata, 4d. com. sh.
———— hypericifolia, var. 6d. com. sh.
———— salicifolia, 4d. com. sh.
———— sorbifolia, 1s. com. sh.
———— thalictroides, 5s. Amer. sh.
———— tomentosa, 1s. 6d. Amer. sh.
Staphylea pinnata, 6d. com. sh.
———— trifolia, 6d. com. sh.
Stuartia malacodendron, 10s. 6d. Amer. sh.
———— Marilandica, 7s. 6d. Amer. sh.
Styrax grandifolia, 10s. 6d. Amer. sh.
———— lævigata, 2s. 6d. Amer. sh.
———— latifolia, 5s. Amer. sh.
Syringa alba, 6d. com. sh.
———— Chinensis, var. 1s. 6d. com. sh.
———— Persica, 6d. com. sh.
———— Siberica, 1s. 6d. com. sh.
———— vulgaris, 6d. com. sh.
———— vulgaris violacea, 6d. com. sh.
Tamarix Gallica, 6d. com. sh.
———— Germanica, 6d. com. sh.
Taxus baccata, 6d. to 2s. 6d. com. ev. sh.
Teucrum flavum, 1s. 6d. ev. sh.
Theuja occidentalis, 1s. com. ev. sh.
———— orientalis, 2s. 6d. com. ev. sh.
Tilia alba, 2s. 6d. H. T.
———— Americana, 2s. 6d. H. T.
———— Carolina, 1s. H. T.
Ulmus America, 3s. 6d. H. T.
———— nemoralis, 1s. 6d. H. T.

Vaccinium amœnum, 2s. 6d. Am. sh.
———— crassifolium, 5s. ev. sh. Amer.
———— formosum, 6s. Amer. sh.
———— lucidum, 5s. ev. sh. Amer.
———— macrocarpon, 1s. 6d. Amer. sh.
———— myrtillus, 1s. 6d. Amer. sh.
———— oxycoccos, 3s. 6d. Amer. sh.
———— Pennsylvanicum, 10s. 6d. Am. ev.
———— pondosum, 10s. 6d. Amer. sh.
———— resinosum, 7s. 6d. Amer. sh.
———— Siberica, 10s. 6d. Amer. sh.
———— uliginosum, 1s. 6d. Amer. sh.
———— vitis idæa, 1s. 6d. ev. sh.
———— vitis idæa major, 1s. 6d. ev. sh. Am.
Viburnum acerifolium, 1s. 6d. com. sh.
———— Carolinianum, 3s. 6d. Amer. sh.
———— cassinoides, 1s. 6d. Amer. sh.
———— dentatum, 4d. com. sh.
———— levigatum, 1s. ev. sh.
———— lantana, 1s. ev. sh.
———— lentago, 6d. com. sh.
———— lucidum, 1s. com. ev. sh.
———— nudum, 6d. com. sh.
———— opulis, 6d. com. sh.
———— opulus Americana, 4d. com. sh.
———— opulus rosea, com. sh.
———— pubescens, com. sh.
———— prunifolium, 1s. com. sh.
———— tinus, 6d. com. ev. sh.
———— variegatum, 1s. 6d. com. sh.
Vinca major, 6d. ev. sh.
———— minor, 6d. ev. sh.
———— var. 6d. ev. sh.
Yucca flamentosa, 2s. 6d. ev. sh. Amer.
———— variegata, 15s. Amer. sh.
Zanthorhiza apifolia, 1s. 6d. Amer. sh.
Zanthoxylum clava Herculis, 1s. com. sh.

(69)

Trees 5 to 6 feet, by the 100.

Elms, Planes, Mountain Ash, Limes, English Oaks, Laburnum, Turkey Oak, Ash, Spanish Chesnut, Birch, Hornbeams, Acacias; from 30s. to 3l. 3s. per 100.

Evergreens, by the 100.

Box, 50s.

Laurels, 30s.

Lauristinus, 30s.

Portugal laurels, 50s.

Hollies, 30s.

Common Shrubs, 30s. per 100.

Collection of Roses, 10l. to 15l.

The following useful Trees, by the 100.

Sycamore, 3 feet, 12s.

H. Chesnuts, 2 to 3 feet, 12s.

Birch, 3 feet, 8s.

Hornbeam, 3 feet, 16s.

Spanish Chesnuts, 2 to 3 feet, 12s.

Beech, 1 to 2 feet, 8s.

Ash, 2 to 3 feet, 8s.

Planes, 3 feet, 30s.

English Oaks, 3 feet, 12s.

Mountain Ash, 3 feet, 12s.

Limes, 3 feet, 30s.

English Elms, 3 to 5 feet, 30s.

Scotch Elms, 3 to 5 feet, 12s.

Firs, 1½ to 2 feet, 6s.

Weymouth Pine, 1½ to 2 feet, 12s.

Spruce Fir, 1 foot, 16s.

Spruce Fir, 1¼ to 2 feet, 25s.

Larch, 2 to 3 feet, 8s.

Alder, 3 feet, 8s

Laburnum, 3 feet, 12s.

Turkey Oaks, 3 feet, 30s.

Acacias, 3 to 4 feet, 25s.

Herbaceous Plants, 3d. to 1s. each, generally 4d. or per 100, 25s.

Fruit Trees.

Maidens, that is, plants one year grafted, are understood, excepting where the contrary is mentioned.

Apple, Standards, 9d. to 1s. 6d.

——— Dwarfs, upon Crab stocks, 8d. to 1s. 4d.

——— Dwarf, upon Paradise stocks, 9d. to 1s. 6d.

Pears, Standards, 1s. 8d. to 3s. 4d.

——— Dwarfs, trained, 2s. 6d. to 5s.

——— Dwarfs, 1s. 3d. to 2s. 6d.

Cherries, Standards, 1s. 8d. to 3s. 4d.

——— Dwarfs, trained,

Cherries, Dwarfs, 1s. 3d. to 2s. 6d.

Plums, Standards, 1s. 3d. to 3s.

——— Dwarfs, trained, 2s. 6d. to 5s.

——— Dwarfs, 1s. 3d. to 2s. 6d.

Quinces, Portugal Standards, 1s. 8d. to 3s. 4d.

——— Dwarfs, 1s. 3d. to 2s. 6d.

Medlars, Dutch, Standards, 1s. 8d. to 3s. 4d.

——— Dwarfs, 1s. 3d. to 2s. 6d.

Apricots, Standards, trained, 3s. 6d. to 7s.

Apricots, Dwarfs, trained, 3s. to 6s.

———— Dwarfs, Maiden plants, 1s. 6d. to 3s.

Peaches, Standards, trained, 7s. 6d. to 15s.

———— Dwarfs, trained, 6s. to 8s.

———— Dwarfs, Maiden plants, 1s. 6d. to 3s.

———— Dwarfs, French kinds, 2s. 6d. to 5s.

Nectarines, Standards, trained, 7s. 6d. to 15s.

———— Dwarfs, trained, 5s. to 10s.

———— Dwarfs, Maiden plants, 1s. 6d. to 3s.

Nectarines, Dwarfs, French kinds, 2s. 6d. to 5s.

Mulberries, Standards, 5s. to 10s.

———— Dwarfs, 1s. 6d. to 3s.

Vines, in pots, 2s. 6d. to 5s.

—— in sorts, 1s. 6d. to 2s. 6d.

Fig trees, in sorts, 6d. to 1s.

Filberts and Spanish nuts, 3d. to 6d.

Gooseberries, in sorts, 2d. to 4d.

———— newest sorts, 6d. to 1s.

Currants, White, Red, }
Black and Champagne, } 2d. to 4d.

F I N I S.

BOOKS

ON

GARDENING, PLANTING, AND RURAL AFFAIRS,

PRINTED FOR JOHN HARDING,

36, St. JAMES'S STREET, LONDON.

MILLER'S GARDENER'S and BOTANIST'S DICTIONARY, containing the best and newest methods of cultivating and improving the Kitchen, Fruit, and Flower Garden, and Nursery, of performing the practical parts of Agriculture, of managing Vineyards, and of propagating all sorts of Timber Trees. A new Edition, enlarged, with the addition of all the Modern Improvements in Landscape Gardening, &c. &c. with Plates, by THOMAS MARTYN, Professor of Botany in the University of Cambridge. 4 vols. folio, price 14l. 14s.

LOUDON'S TREATISE on FORMING, IMPROVING, and MANAGING COUNTRY RESI-DENCES, including the Construction and Arrangement of Rural Buildings, and the Formation of Gardens, Parks, and Farms, &c. &c. Illustrated by Descriptions of Scenery and Buildings, by reference to Country Seats and Passages of Country, in most parts of Great Britain, and by Thirty-two Plates. 2 vols. 4to. 3l. 3s.

MADOCK'S FLORIST'S DIRECTORY, a complete Treatise on the Culture and Management of the principal Flowers and Bulbous Roots; with Instructions for the Composition of Manures, Earths, and Composts, and for performing the different Operations of Horticulture; a new Edition, improved, by Curtis, and illustrated with coloured Plates of the Flowers, Implements of Gardening, &c. 8vo. price 21s. and a few superior Copies, 31s. 6d.

MARSHALL'S PRACTICAL TREATISE on PLANTING and RURAL ORNAMENT, con-taining a Dictionary of Trees, Shrubs, and Plants, with Instructions for Forming Plantations, &c. &c. 2 vols. 8vo. A new Edit. 16s.

PONTEY'S TREATISE on PLANTING and FOREST PRUNING, with an Essay on the Management of Oak Woods. With Plates. 2 vols. price 21s.

GANDY'S DESIGNS for COTTAGES, FARM HOUSES, LODGES, ENTRANCE GATES, and other Country Buildings, with Ground Plans, Descriptions, and Estimates. 4to. Forty-three Plates, 2l. 2s.

Pl. 1

Pl. 2

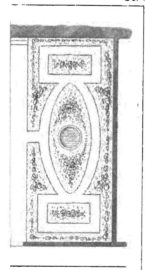

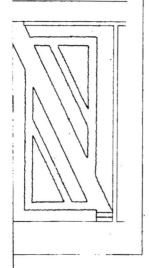

Pl. 3.

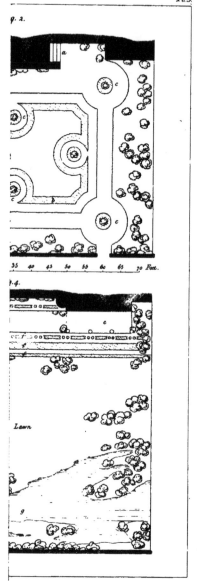

q. 2.

a

c

c

c

b

c

c

35   40   45   50   55   60   65   70 Feet.

.4.

c

f

Lawn

g

Pl.4.

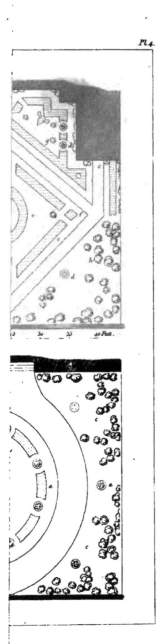

Pl.5.

F.3.

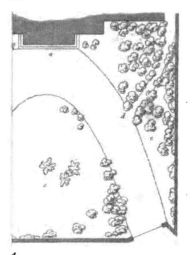

4.

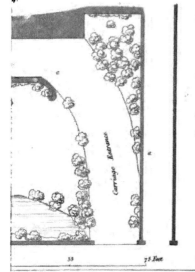

Carriage Entrance

75 Feet.

Pl. 6

Park

Park

Fig. 2.   *Pl. 7.*

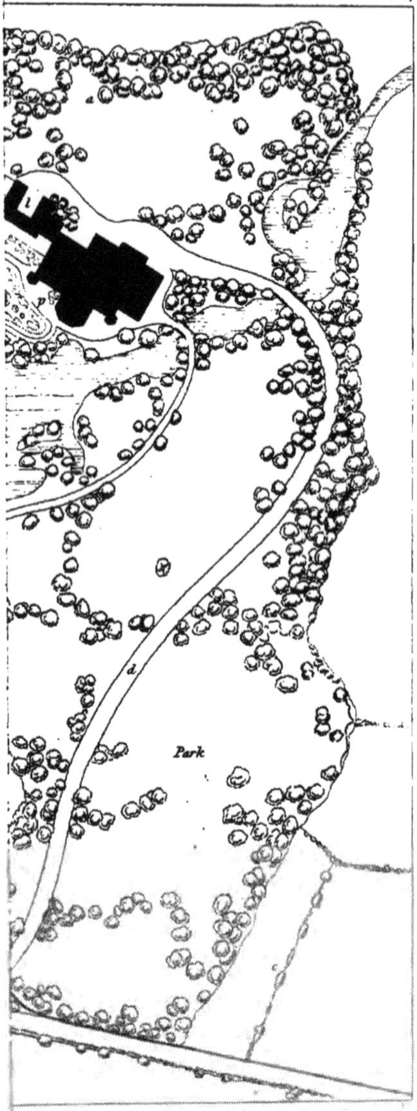

Park

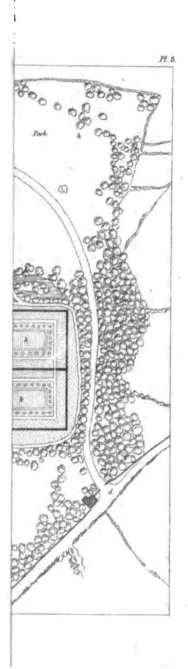

Pl. 9

Pl.10.

Pl. II.

Pl.12.

Fig. 4.

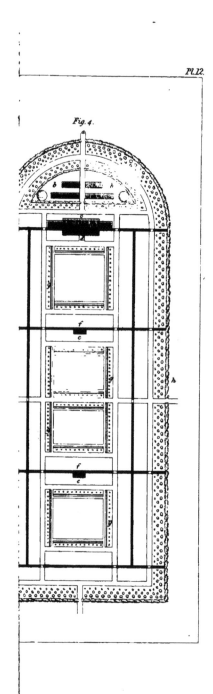

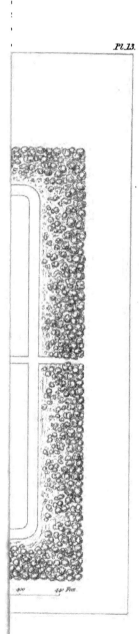

Pl. 13.

Pl.14.

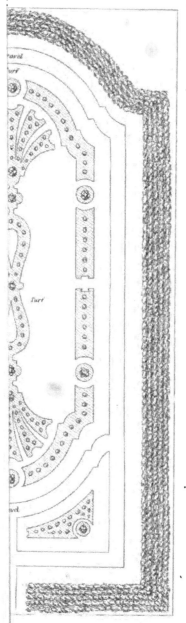

Pl.15.

Pl. 16

Parterre.

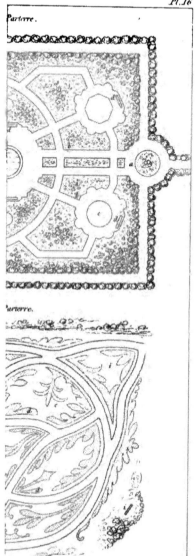

Parterre.

Pl. 16

Parterre.

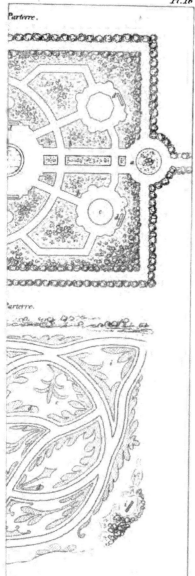

Parterre.

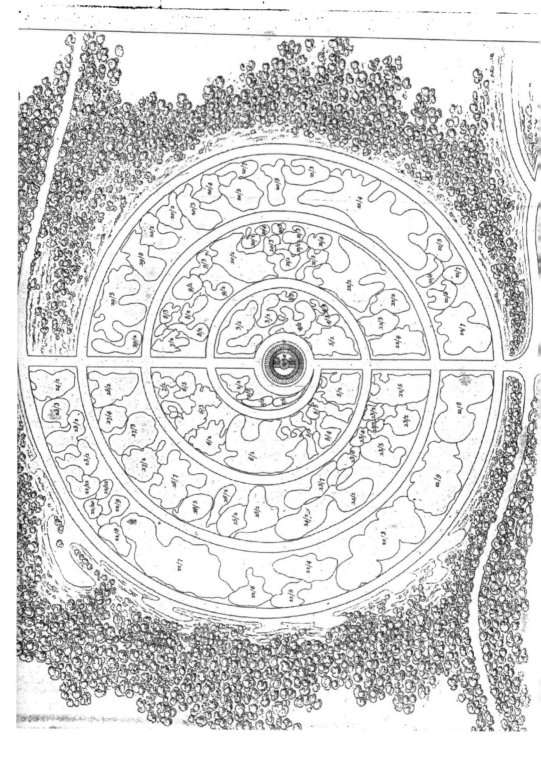

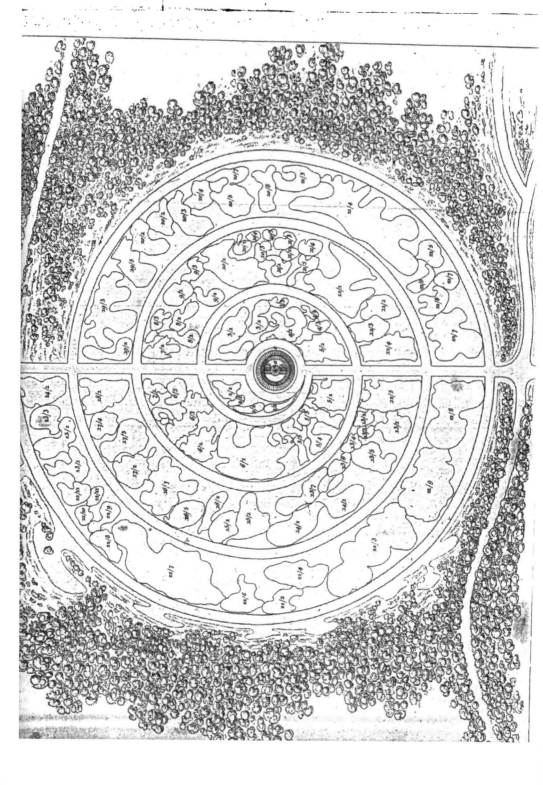

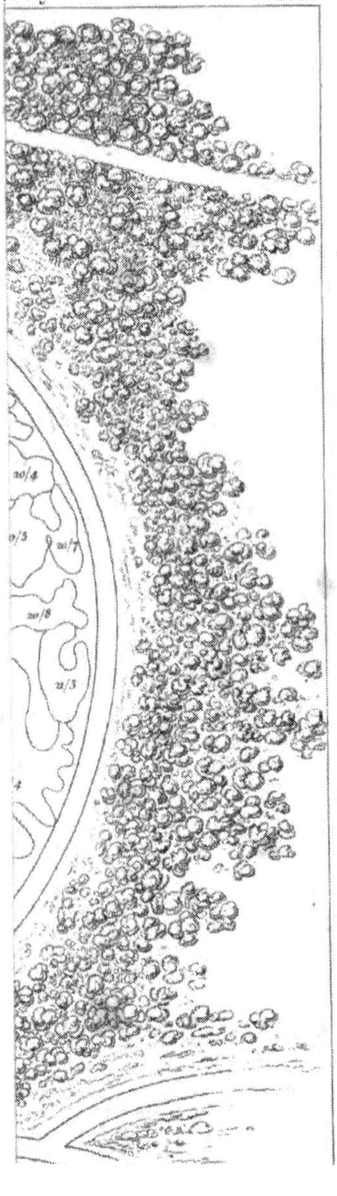
w/4
w/7
w/8
u/3

Pl.28.

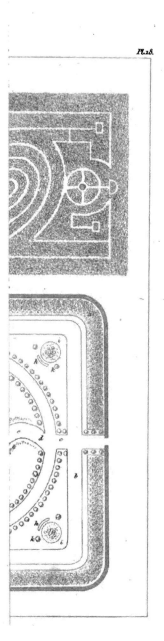

Pl.19.

&c

e

c

d

c

60   70   80 Feet.

Pl. 20.

Sect. o..d

Lightning Source UK Ltd.
Milton Keynes UK
UKHW020637280421
382769UK00004B/204